Clan Ewen

Some Records of its History

Clan Ewen
Some Records of its History

R. S. T. MacEwen

*A New Facsimile Edition
with Notes and Commentary
by John Thor Ewing
Commander of Clan Ewing*

WELKIN BOOKS

Clan Ewen: Some records of its history first published by the Office of *The Celtic Monthly*, John Mackay, Glasgow 1904

First Published in this edition 2016
Welkin Books Ltd

This edition copyright © Welkin Books Ltd 2016
All Notes and Introduction Copyright © Thor Ewing 2016
Thor Ewing asserts his right to be identified as author in accordance with the Design, Copyrights and Patents Act 1988

All rights reserved. No part of this publication may be reproduced, stored in a retrieval system, or transmitted in any form or by any means, without the prior written permission of the publisher, nor be otherwise circulated in any from of binding or cover other than that in which it is published and without a similar condition being imposed upon the subsequent purchaser.

ISBN 978-1-910075-04-3

Acknowledgements

I have received help from many sources and hope that I do not inadvertently offend anyone through their accidental ommission. Many more people have been involved with other aspects of the clan, and it's not always possible to separate the two but, the people mentioned below have all offered help and support, or contributed to an aspect of historical research behind this book: Sir John and Lady McEwen of Marchmont and Bardrochat; Andrew McEwen of Ballinreoch; Euan MacLachlan of MacLachlan; Robin and Fiona Maclean of Ardgour; David Sellar; Professor Jane Dawson; Ronald Black; Dr Mark Jardine; Diane Baptie; Hugh Peskett; Jim McMichael; Alan Milliken; Bill Riddle; Christian Orr Ewing; Beth Ewing Toscos; Joe Neff Ewing; Colin Davies; Malcolm McEwan; Barry R. McCain; Bob McLaughlin; Hugh MacDougall; Tom McLachlan; Ken Godfrey; Nan Beams; Jeanne Bickford; Steve Ewing; Lance Ewing; Sandy Alexander; Susan Hedeen; Jean Brittain; John McKown; John D. McLaughlin; Peter Mennie of the Highland Archive Centre; Olive Geddes of the National Library of Scotland; Tessa Spencer of the National Register of Archives for Scotland; and Jennifer Duffy of National Records of Scotland.

Special thanks are due to David Neal Ewing, Thomas Ashby McCown and Dr Bruce Durie, who have read and commented on earlier drafts of the text. I must also acknowledge the support of both my immediate family and the wider clan, which has been invaluable.

As always, responsibility for errors rests with me alone.

Introduction

Since its first publication in 1904, this book (alongside brief accounts derived from it) has been almost the sole guide for many MacEwens and Ewings, Cowans and McEwings, as they try to understand their ancestry in relation to the Scottish clans. Through online editions and modern reprints, R. S. T. MacEwen's work is now more readily available than ever before, and it is still taken on trust by people hoping to explore their MacEwen ancestry. Regrettably, one of the most important tasks of this new edition will be to show why that trust is, at least in some respects, misplaced.

R. S. T. MacEwen's work first appeared in the pages of *The Celtic Monthly* (Vol.VI, 1898, and Vol.VII, 1899) and, at the time of his death in June 1900, he was planning to expand and revise these articles for publication in book form. Perhaps, if he had lived to properly revise his earlier articles for re-publication as a book, R. S. T. MacEwen would himself have corrected many of the errors detailed in my notes below. As he did not, these errors have remained uncorrected, so that not only amateur enthusiasts but subsequent writers have too often mistaken them for fact.

There is also a good deal that is of genuine interest in R. S. T. MacEwen's work and although, for reasons of necessity, I have concentrated in my notes on tackling problems, I hope that I have not entirely overlooked his successes. R. S. T. MacEwen's enthusiasm for his clan is laudable, and it's clear that he purposefully established correspondence with several MacEwens he believed could shed light on their family histories. Without his dedication, the knowledge of R. S. T. MacEwen's correspondents would certainly have been lost for ever. Specifically, the traditions recounted by Mr. John McEwen (p14-8) which have helped establish the ancestry of the Galloway McEwens would have been lost, as would the peculiar and enchanting legend of the white horse (p28) which was recorded from an old soldier probably born in the 1760's. In my own clan, we would have lost the knowledge that the grant of arms, recorded in an obscure document of

1566, was remembered because of the new clan banner it entailed (p12-3) —the realisation that this memory, along with the sense of clanship it embodies, was passed down by word of mouth through the centuries is breathtaking. Whatever his shortcomings in interpreting these traditions, we owe R. S. T. MacEwen a debt of gratitude for their very preservation and, because of the unique record he provided of these diverse traditions, his work now takes the place of a primary source for these oral histories.

But if R. S. T. MacEwen recorded the traditions of these different clans and families, he also denied their separate identities. Much of his book is taken up with the frequent repetition of his personal belief that all MacEwens are descended from a single clan—in this, he was plainly mistaken. Although for some readers, R. S. T. MacEwen's vision of a single united MacEwen history may seem superficially attractive, in the end it is deeply unsatisfactory. It replaces the relatively coherent stories of several distinct and separate MacEwen families with a synthesis of stories from many unconnected histories, and the result is incoherence and confusion.

Different MacEwen clans appear to have been carefully distinguished in medieval times. The designation 'of Otter' in the genealogy for Clan Ewen of Otter in 1467MS, suggests the genealogist was concerned to differentiate them from other MacEwen clans which did not share the same ancestry. Although written down at a date after 1467, this genealogy seems not to have been updated after the chiefship of Walter V who died before 1410. Other MacEwen clans in existence at this date probably included the Galloway McEwens (see note "the Black Douglas" p15), the MacPhersons and the Macleans of Ardgour (see note "Mackintosh genealogies" p28), and perhaps the MacEwens of Clan MacDougall (see note "Perthshire" p28). No other clan in 1467MS is distinguished from similarly-named clans in this way, which suggests the existence of several clans of the name MacEwen may have been recognised as a potential problem by contemporaries.

R. S. T. MacEwen's belief in the 'dispersion' of Clan Ewen of Otter was founded upon a fundamental misreading of a passage in Keltie, which actually relates to Siol Gillevray, a hypothetical grouping of clans with no real connection to Clan Ewen of Otter. He had also clearly trawled through a great many history books, picking out the MacEwen name wherever it occurred but, in this approach he shows a basic misunderstanding of the distinction between the use of MacEwen as a genuine clan name and as a patronymic. Indeed, he was not merely confused by the similarity between patronymics and clan names, but he based whole sections of his argument upon his confusion. So although R. S. T. MacEwen cited various historical documents which give the illusion of supporting evidence, these references are either irrelevant, misunderstood, or both.

At the heart of R. S. T. MacEwen's version of history lies the extraordinary suggestion that a relatively small clan might not only survive for five hundred years without any of the usual appurtenances of clanship—most importantly without a chief—but would actually grow and expand until it represented one of the most numerous names in all Scotland. The unlikely inference would appear to be that, if only other clans had not been encumbered with lands and chiefs, they too could have prospered like the MacEwens.

As will be seen from the notes below, Clan Ewen of Otter does seem to have lived on in another guise, but it did not expand. After relocating from Loch Fyne to Loch Lomond, it apparently remained a coherent clan in the reign of Mary, Queen of Scots, when its chief was awarded a grant of arms, and it mustered to fight at the Battle of Langside in 1568; its descendants today are usually known not by the name of MacEwen but of Ewing. All evidence suggests that the large bodies of MacEwens indigenous to other parts of the country have other origins. In broad terms: McEwens from Galloway would seem to be descended ultimately from Clan Bisset, and to have arrived from Ireland with their allies the Agnews in the fourteenth century; McEwans in Perthshire and around Loch Tay, along with their cousins in Argyll and Lorne, are descended from Clan MacDougall; further north, other MacEwans are apparently descended from Clan Cameron's *Sliochd Eoghain mhic Eoghain*, and there might also be a number of MacEwens who belong with Clan Chattan. All these MacEwen origins are witnessed by historical evidence, but there is no genuine evidence for the supposed origin of the modern surname MacEwen in the medieval Clan Ewen of Otter except in relation to Dumbartonshire. These various MacEwen clans and families are not connected in any meaningful way with Clan Ewen of Otter, and it would be disingenuous to pretend otherwise. However, there is no single MacEwen origin which represents the 'real' MacEwens—if you are a MacEwen, then whichever clan your ancestors belonged to represents your true history.

Curiously, there may have been a particular reason why R. S. T. MacEwen was predisposed to believe in the common descent of MacEwens from Clan Ewen of Otter. From his obituary published in *The Celtic Monthly* (No.7 Vol.IX, April 1901), we can see that R. S. T. MacEwen was descended from a Walter MacEwen (or McEwan) in Luss. The Luss McEwans claimed a long-standing association with the area and kept alive clan traditions stretching back to the sixteenth century, yet it is the Ewing form which clearly predominates in early records for Dumbartonshire, and these McEwan traditions are supported by records in the Ewing name (p12-3). Gaelic was the language of Luss in the early nineteenth century, and the Gaelic form of the name always remained *Mac Eoghain*, so it is not surprising that one or two family lines might have entered the records as McEwans rather than as Ewings.

Presumably, when Walter's grandson, Dr Alexander McEwan, moved north to Sutherland, he adopted the local spelling of the name and became a MacEwen. Thus, his son Robert came to grow up with the traditions of a clan from Dumbartonshire and a spirit of kinship with MacEwens in Sutherland. Later in life when Robert came to research the history of his clan, his lifelong belief in the common identity of all MacEwen clans was so deeply entrenched that he was oblivious to all evidence to the contrary. When he investigated his own clan in the area of Loch Lomond, he saw the Ewing surname which he thought had its origin in 'special or fanciful reasons' (p30), and the Ewing armorial tradition which he mistakenly believed to be derived from an unrelated Lowland family (p34). Had he looked again, perhaps he would have realised that it was this clan alone which could fairly claim to represent the heirs to Clan Ewen of Otter as told in his family tradition.

In an entirely unrelated blunder, the historian William Forbes Skene commented in 1847 that Clan Ewen of Otter 'seems to have been a branch of the Clan Lauchlan' (*Collectanea de Rebus Albanicis*). Skene's error was given further impetus when it was picked up by Frank Adam in his influential book, *The Clans Septs & Regiments of the Scottish Highlands* (1908, p329). Accordingly, Clan Ewen of Otter was wrongly categorised as a branch of Clan MacLachlan. In keeping with R. S. T. MacEwen's claim that all MacEwens represent a single clan, this case of mistaken identity has been applied to Ewings and MacEwens equally, so that Clan MacLachlan societies have opened their arms to welcome MacEwens descended from Clan Bisset, Clan MacDougall and Clan Cameron.

Both MacEwens and Ewings have found friendship and fellowship in MacLachlan societies, and it would be churlish not to appreciate the positive role played by other clans in our recent history. My aim in writing these notes is not to stand in the way of a spirit of comradeship between us and others who share a similar name, or with comrades from other unrelated clans. We are all Jock Tamson's bairns, after all. But having now identified the mistakes of the past, we have a duty to ensure that future generations are not compelled to repeat them unnecessarily.

In 2014, after a joint Family Convention or *Derbhfine*, Lord Lyon acknowledged the separate histories and traditions of Ewings and MacEwens when he recognised their existence as two distinct clans and appointed a separate Commander for each clan. I am privileged to have been appointed as commander of Clan Ewing, while Clan MacEwen is focussed around the family of Colmonell, Ayrshire, in the person of its commander, Sir John McEwen of Marchmont and Bardrochat, Bt. Sir John's grandfather, Sir John McEwen, 1ˢᵗ Baronet (1894-1962), served as M.P. for Berwick and Haddington from 1931 to 1945, and was described by Sir Iain Moncrieffe of that Ilk as 'one of the finest and most talented Scottish gentlemen of our day' (1967, 1982, *The Highland Clans*, p137)—he was the son of Robert Finnie McEwen of Bardrochat, Deputy Lieutenant of Ayrshire, who registered arms in 1908.

I understand from Mr. Andrew McEwen of Ballinreoch, who claims descent from John Mackewan of Muckley, that he plans to reaffirm his family's traditional allegiance to Clan MacDougall as a direct descendant of the chieftains of the MacEwens of Clan MacDougall. This was a very significant sept which probably accounts for the great majority of Highland MacEwens in Perthshire, Argyll and Lorne (see note "Perthshire" below, p28). Although his family have faithfully preserved traditions stretching back to Culloden and beyond, like so many other MacEwen families, they had become persuaded that they were descended from Clan Ewen of Otter, and only recently rediscovered their true genealogy preserved in the records of Lyon Court tracing their line to the MacDougall chiefs.

History is the groundwork for our relationship with the past, but it is a matter for each of us as individuals to choose how we honour our heritage and preserve it for the next generation. All these groups, Clan MacEwen, Clan MacDougall, Clan MacLachlan and Clan Ewing, continue to extend a fraternal hand in a spirit of fellowship to everyone of every surname who wishes to pursue their heritage through their clan, and I have no doubt that any MacEwen tracing their roots to an origin in another clan, whether to Clan Cameron, Clan Chattan or to a hitherto unsuspected origin, will find an equal welcome among their kinsfolk there.

Whatever clan your ancestors might have pledged allegiance to, or even shed blood for, I hope you will find these notes both useful and interesting, and that they might help you better to understand the possible origins of your own family.

J. T. E.

History of Clan Ewen.

I. The Dalriada Scots.

THE ancient Clan Ewen or MacEwen of Otter, Eoghan na h-Oitrich, which once possessed a stronghold of its own, was one of the earliest of the western clans sprung from the Dalriada Scots. These Scots were among the assailants of the Roman province in Britain, but they did not finally settle in Argyllshire till the beginning of the sixth century. The year 503 is usually said to mark the commencement of the reign of their first king in Argyllshire; but little of their history is known prior to the foundation of the Scottish Monarchy in the middle of the ninth century. Skene thinks they came more as colonists than invaders. The first leaders were the three sons of Ere—Lorn, Fergus, and Angus. These were the representatives of three or four tribes who frequently fought among themselves, and against the Britons and Saxons. Historians are of opinion that from 736 to 800 they were partly, if not wholly, subject to the Picts.

sprung from the Dalriada Scots - There is no reason to believe that the MacEwens of Otter traced their ancestry to the Kingdom of Dàl Riata as is claimed here. The sole surviving account, which is preserved in a fifteenth-century manuscript commonly known as 1467MS (National Library of Scotland Adv.MS.72.1.1), claims descent from the semi-legendary Anrothan (Anradhan) who is supposed to have arrived from Ireland in the eleventh century (see notes "MacEwen", "Ferchard" below, p4).

Skene - William Forbes Skene (1809-92) was a noted Scottish historian, who brought to light the clan genealogies recorded in 1467MS. He transcribed and published the genealogy of Clan Ewen of Otter in 'Genealogies of the Highland Clans, extracted from Ancient Gaelic MSS,' (*Collectanea de Rebus Albanicis*, 1847) and again in *Celtic Scotland* (3 vols, Edinburgh, 1876-80, Vol.III p474). Modern historians interpret the early history of Dàl Riata somewhat differently from their nineteenth-century predecessors, but the details are not strictly relevant to MacEwen history.

Britons and Saxons - In this context the term 'Briton' refers to the native Brythonic or Cymric people who had occupied most of mainland Britain since before the Romans. In historical times, their northernmost outpost was the Kingdom of Strathclyde, with its capital at Dumbarton. The term 'Saxons' here denotes the Angles, whose northernmost kingdom of Bernicia extended throughout Lothian and, at its height, included Edinburgh as well as territories in south-west Scotland.

St. Columba, who was one of them, established the monastery of Iona in 563 A.D. He was sprung from the Royal House of the Northern Hy Neill, while in the female line he was connected with the Kings of Dalriada. According to Skene, the last of the old abbots of Iona of whom there is any notice died in 1099, and thereafter, for upwards of sixty years, there is an unbroken silence regarding the Monastery. The Celtic Church had to give way before the invasion of one of the religious orders of the Roman Church. In the twelfth century, Somerled, who had Iona for one of his possessions, attempted to restore the old abbey and offered it to the Abbot of Derry, but the Abbot of Armagh and the King of Ireland disallowed the proposal. In 1166, on the succession of his son Reginald, the monastery was re-built on a larger scale. Reginald is said to have been "the most distinguished of the Galls and of the Gaels for prosperity, sway of generosity, and feats of arms"; and the Church benefited largely by these qualities. Adopting the policy of the Scottish Kings he introduced to his territories the religious orders of the Roman Church. He founded three monasteries—one of Black Monks in Iona, in honour of God and St. Columba; one of Black Nuns in the same place; and one of Grey Friars (Cistercian or White Monks) at Saddell in Cantire. It is of this later Roman Catholic Benedictine Monastery and Nunnery,* and not of the Columban buildings, that the present ruins are the remains. The Western Celts continued to be Roman Catholics till the Reformation. But the original Celtic Church in Columba's time was not the Romish Church as represented at the present day. Columba stands forth as

* Skene's "Celtic Scotland," Vol. II.

St Columba - Columba was exiled from Ireland for his role in the Battle of Cúl Dreimhne, and came to Scotland as a missionary where he was granted land on Iona in 563. After his death in 597, his bones remained on the island until 849, when they were removed for safety. His relics were enshrined in the Brecbennoch and, in 1314, they were present at the Battle of Bannockburn.

The Celtic Church ... the Roman Church - After the collapse of the Roman Empire, insular Christians lost touch with Rome so that, by the time the two Churches next came into contact, two distinct traditions had emerged. Key differences concerned the relative primacy of abbots and bishops, the cut of the tonsure, and the dating of Easter.

of the Galls and of the Gaels - In medieval Gaelic, the words *Gall* and *Gàidheil* most often distinguish Norsemen from Gaels, and are used throughout history to distinguish non-Gaelic speakers. Thus, George Buchanan (1506-82) writes, 'the ancient Scots divided all the nations who inhabited Britain, into two classes, the one they called Gael, the other [Gall]' (1827, *The History of Scotland*, p104). By the nineteenth century, the terms commonly distinguish between Lowlanders and Highlanders.

the great founder of the Ionian Church, whence radiated the light which penetrated to England and a great part of the continent of Europe.

Somerled, Regulus of Argyll, was the leader of the Scots in the middle of the twelfth century. He was a son of Gillebride, and grandson of Gille-Adamnan. Gillebride had been driven from the Scottish Dalriada by the Norwegians, and applied for help to his Irish kindred. He returned to Scotland with his son Somerled and a band of followers, who encountered and defeated a large force of Norwegians, and seized their territories. In 1153 the Scots rose against Malcolm IV., but Somerled was detached by an offer of the Isles, while some of his chiefs were imprisoned in Roxburgh Castle. In 1164 he again rose and landed at Renfrew, but he was defeated and slain. He had married a daughter of Olave, the Norwegian King, and left four sons, Dubhgal, Reginald, Angus, and Olave. The eldest succeeded to his father's possessions on the mainland, while the second, Reginald, received the Isles, with the title of King of the Isles. Up to 1222 Argyll maintained semi-independence of the Scottish Crown, and it was not till 1266, in the reign of Alexander III., that the Hebrides and the Western Isles were annexed to the kingdom.

Hill Burton says the Celtic races were Christian when they first settled in Scotland, and had a literary language and a written literature in their own tongue, and were in a higher stage of civilization than the Picts, the Britons, or the Saxons. As to their religion, we know they were under the spiritual sway of Iona. Whatever the cause, there can be no doubt of their success; they came, they saw, they conquered,

Somerled - Somerled (Gaelic, *Somhairlidh*, Old Norse, *Sumarliði*, d.1164) usurped power during the 1150's from his brother-in-law Godred Olafsson, King of the Isles. He was killed during an attempted invasion of Scotland. Although early historians cast him as a hero of Gaelic resistance against Scandinavian domination, DNA study would suggest that Somerled was also of Norse paternal ancestry (Bryan Sykes and Jayne Nicholson, 'The Genetic Structure of a Highland Clan').

Hill Burton - John Hill Burton, 1873, *The History of Scotland; from Agricola's invasion to the extinction of the last Jacobite insurrection*. Although it was once commonplace to speak of 'Celtic races', modern historians consider Celtic identity as a matter of language and cultural affiliation—both Picts and Britons would usually be grouped alongside the Gaels among the 'Celtic' nations of history. Any assessment of the relative degree of civilisation among past nations is necessarily subjective, but the cultural sophistication of the early Gaels should not be underestimated. It is no longer believed that the Scottish Gaels took Caledonia by conquest, and indigenous populations of the Scottish regions today partly reflect ancient patterns of settlement.

they settled and spread, and eventually gave their name to the kingdom—Scotland.

II. THE MACEWENS OF OTTER.
CLANN EOGHAIN NA H-OITRICH.

Up to the thirteenth century these Scots were divided into a few great tribes, corresponding to the ancient maormorships or earldoms. Skene, in his "Table of the Descent of the Highland Clans," divides the Gallgael into five great clans, from whom sprung nine smaller clans. The clan system of later times had not appeared before this date. From the Siol Gillevray, the second of the great clans, he gives the Clans Neill, Lachlan, and Ewen: Chiefs MacNeill, MacLachlan, and MacEwen. He shows the Clan Lamond to have sprung from Siol Eachern, although elsewhere it would appear that Ferchard and Ewen, the ancestors of the Lamonds and MacEwens, were brothers. The genealogies given by Skene are taken from the Irish MSS. and Mac Firbis. He considers the later portion of the pedigrees, as far back as the common ancestor from whom the clan takes its name, to be tolerably well vouched for, and it may be held to be authentic.

Referring to the Maclachlans, MacEwens, and Lamonds, he says, "this group brings us nearer historical times. They are sprung from Aodha Alain, termed Buirche, called by Keltie De Dalan. This Aodha Alain, or De Dalan, was the son of Anradan, and grandson of Aodha Allamuin (Hugh Allaman), the then head of the great family of O'Neils, kings of Ireland, descended from Niall Glundubh, and the

five great clans - Skene's 'Table of the Descent of the Highland Clans' appears on p373 of *The Highlanders of Scotland* (1837). At this stage of his research, Skene believed that a group of clans was descended from a Gillebride whose name he saw in a number of genealogies in 1467MS, and he named this group 'Siol Gillevray'. Skene's division into five clan groups is no longer used, and more recent historians have preferred to consider groups acknowledged in early sources. The tenth-century *Senchus fer n-Alban* lists three great kindreds for Dàl Riata: *Cenèl nGabràin* (in Kintyre), *Cenèl nÒengusa* (in Islay and Jura), and *Cenèl Loairn* (in Lorne, and perhaps also in Mull and Ardnamurchan), with a fourth kindred, *Cenèl Comgaill* (in Cowal and Bute) being added later (*Senchus fer n-Alban* translated by John Bannerman, *Studies in the History of Dalriada*, Scottish Academic Press, p47-9; previously published in *Celtica*, Vols.VII-IX 1966-1971).

MacEwen - The genealogy of Clan Ewen of Otter survives only in the manuscript presented by Skene known as 1467MS (see notes "sprung from the Dalriada Scots" & "Skene" above, p1). Skene's placing of Clan Ewen of Otter in Siol Gillevray (see note "five great clans" above) is apparently based on his reading of the Lamont genealogy in 1467MS which he at first believed traced the line of Anrothan through 'Gilbert king of the Western Isles' to 'Neillgusa of Lochaber' but, in the words of its most recent editor, 'There are no such people in the Lamont pedigree' (Ronald Black, 2013, '1467MS: The Lamonts' *West Highland Notes & Queries*, Ser.III No.21 p3-19). In 1837, Skene referred to 'Anradan Mac Gillebride' but by 1890, when he published the third volume of *Celtic Scotland*, Skene had clearly realised his error, and it is not possible that he would still have grouped Clan Ewen of Otter with the clans of Siol Gillevray.

Ferchard - The genealogy for Clan Ewen of Otter in 1467MS is barely legible in places, but it seems that this 'Ferchard' (or *Fearchar*) is likely to have been the grandfather of the first Ewen of Otter. Based on recent scholarship by Ronald Black, the text of the genealogy can now be rendered as: 'The genealogy of MacEwen of Otter here: Walter (Bhaltair) son of John (Eoin) son of Ewen (Eoghan) son of Archibald (Gilleasbaig) son of Ewen (Eoghan) son of Duncan (Donnchadh) [son] of this [unnamed] son of Baron Dunsleve (Donnsleibhe) son of handsome Hugh (Aodh) who is called the Buirrce son of Anrothan (Anradhan) son of Flaherty (Flaithbheartach)' (this translation is based on the work of Ronald Black in '1467 MS. The MacEwens', *West Highland Notes & Queries*, Ser. 3, no. 24, Jan 2014, pp. 15-22). Through comparison with other sources, most importantly the appearance of Dunsleve's grandson Lauman alongside his uncle 'Duncan son of Farquhar' in a charter of about 1235 in the *Register of the Monastery of Paisley*, it is possible with a fair degree of confidence to identify the unnamed son of Dunsleve as Farquhar or 'Ferchard' (Gaelic, *Fearchar*).

Irish MSS - Using other Gaelic genealogies preserved in Irish sources, the family tree can be traced back into the realms of legend. Opinion is divided as to how much credence can be given to such evidence. Whilst it is certain that the medieval Gaelic genealogies are often flawed, some scholars believe they might nonetheless preserve genuine traditions from ancient times, while others regard the whole system as pure invention. Some have questioned the historicity of Anrothan (Anradhan) who is almost unknown outside Gaelic genealogical lists but, although there is genuine room for doubt, it would be unwise to dismiss the testimony of the genealogies out of hand on this point. Skene's trust in the later sections of the genealogies is still generally considered to be well founded.

Mac Firbis - Duald Mac Firbis (Dubhaltach MacFhirbhisigh) was a seventeenth-century Irish writer, historian and genealogist.

Keltie - John Scott Keltie, 1875, *A History of the Scottish Highlands, Highland Clans and Scottish Regiments*.

Niall Glundubh - Niall Glúndub (King of Aileach 911-19, High King of Ireland 915-917, d.919), progenitor of the O'Neill dynasty of Ulster, chiefs of Cenél nEógain.

fabulous King Conn of the one hundred battles." Niall Glundubh lived between 850 and 900.

Aodha Alain, whose death is recorded in 1047, had three sons: Gillachrist, Neill, and Dunslebhe. Gillachrist had a son, Lachlan, who was the ancestor of the Maclachlans; Neill was the ancestor of the MacNeills. Dunslebhe had two sons, Ferchard, ancestor of the Lamonds, and Ewen, ancestor of the MacEwens. The four were kindred tribes; but if Ferchard and Ewen were brothers, the Lamonds and MacEwens were originally more closely allied to each other than they were to the Maclachlans and MacNeills. "These clans were in possession, in the twelfth century, of the greater part of the district of Cowal, from Toward Point to Strachur. The Lamonds were separated from the MacEwens by the river Kilfinnan, and the MacEwens from the Maclachlans by the stream which divides the parishes of Kilfinnan and Strath Lachlan. The MacNeills took possession of the islands of Barra and Gigha."*

The MacEwens possessed a tract of country about twenty-five miles square, and could probably bring out 200 fighting men. "On the conquest of Argyll by Alexander II., 1222, they suffered severely, and were involved in the ruin which overtook all the adherents of Somerled, except the MacNeills, who consented to hold their lands of the Crown, and the Maclachlans, who gained their former consequence by means of marriage with the heiress of the Lamonds."* But although the MacEwens suffered severely at this time, a remnant survived under their own chief at Otter, on the shores of Loch Fyne, where the last chief died two-and-a-half centuries afterwards.

*Keltie, *History of the Highland Clans*, Vol. ii.

Ewen, ancestor of the MacEwens - The suggestion that the Clan Ewen of Otter is descended from Ewen son of Dunsleve would appear to be at odds with the only surviving genealogy as recorded in 1467MS, which traces descent from 'Ewen son of Duncan [son] of this son of Baron Dunsleve.' An unrelated source allows us to identify the 'son of Baron Dunsleve' as Farquhar (Gaelic, *Fearchar*; see note "Ferchard" above, p4).

a tract of country about twenty-five miles square - Perhaps MacEwen means twenty five square miles, a very much smaller area equivalent to five miles square, which is roughly the size of the Barony of Otter.

200 fighting men - It is not clear how R. S. T. MacEwen has arrived at this figure.

These clans were in possession - John Scott Keltie, 1875, *History of the Scottish Highlands, Highland Clans and Regiments*, Vol.V p166.

On the conquest of Argyll by Alexander II. - Here Keltie (Vol.II, p162) is closely following James Browne, 1840, *A history of the Highlands and of the Highland Clans*, Vol.IV p451, who in turn is following Skene, 1837, *The Highlanders of Scotland*, Vol.II p114. Neither Skene, Browne nor Keltie were in fact discussing Clan Ewen of Otter at this point, but Skene's 'Siol Gillevray' (see note "five great clans" above, p4). R. S. T. MacEwen returns repeatedly to this point, seeming to believe that these earlier historians really thought Clan Ewen of Otter had fragmented in the fifteenth century, whereas in fact they were discussing events which occurred long before this clan ever existed. As Browne says, even the association of Clan Ewen of Otter with Siol Gillevray is 'questionable' (see note "MacEwen" above, p4).

As quoted here, although not in its original context, this passage appears to suggest that it was Clan Ewen of Otter which 'suffered severely' through Alexander II's conquest, and we would infer that the clan was already in existence at the time and was supporting Somerled. However, neither of these inferences would be correct. By 1222, Somerled had been dead for nearly sixty years, so the inhabitants of Cowal cannot be considered as his 'adherents' at this date. Neither is it possible that Clan Ewen of Otter was already in existence at this date, since 'Duncan son of Farquhar', father of the original Ewen of Otter, appears in a charter of about 1235 in the *Register of the Monastery of Paisley*.

Ewen Mor MacDougall, King of the Isles, may have opposed Alexander II in later campaigns against Argyll, but is not connected with Clan Ewen of Otter (see note "Perthshire", below p28).

MacEwen I. of Otter, the earliest chief of the clan of whom there is any mention, flourished about 1200. He was succeeded by Severan II. of Otter, who was probably the chief of 1222. The names of the third and fourth chiefs are lost. Gillespie V. of Otter assumed the chiefship about 1315. From this date there were four chiefs; Ewen VI., John VII., Walter VIII., and Sufnee or Swene, the IX. and last of the Otter chiefs. So late as 1750 it is recorded in the "Old Statistical Account of the Parish of Kilfinnan":—"On a rocky point on Loch Fyne there stood in 1700 the ruins of Castle MacEwen (Caisteal MhicEoghain), the stronghold of the earlier lords of the Otter." On the same authority, quoted by Skene, this MacEwen is described as the chief of the clan and proprietor of the northern division of the parish of Otter, and in the MS. of 1450, which contains the genealogy of Clann Eoghain na h-Oitrich, or Clan Ewen, the MacEwens are derived from Anradan, the common ancestor of the MacLachlans and the MacNeills.

In 1431-32 Swene MacEwen, IX. of Otter, granted a charter of certain lands of Otter to Duncan, son of Alexander Campbell. In 1432 he resigned the barony of Otter to James I., but received it anew from the king with remainder to Celestine Campbell, son and heir of Duncan Campbell of Lochow. After Swene's death, King James, in 1493, confirmed the grant to Archibald, Earl of Argyll, as heir to his father, Colin. In 1513 the barony of Otter was confirmed to Earl Colin by James V. In 1526 it was resigned by Earl Colin, and granted by James V. to Archibald, his son and heir apparent. In 1575 another Archibald Campbell appears in a charter as "of the Otter"; and in the Act of 1587 a Campbell is entered as "The Laird of

MacEwen I. of Otter - The genealogy recorded in 1467MS, which is our sole record for the early history of this clan, makes no mention of this 'MacEwen' and since no evidence is cited for his existence, it is impossible to know who is meant. 'MacEwen' means 'son of Ewen', so we should expect MacEwen's father Ewen to have been the founder of the clan and to have flourished in the last quarter of the twelfth century. This would be surprisingly early for the foundation of the clan but, in any case, as there would appear to be no evidence for the existence of this Ewen, we must discount him.

Severan II. of Otter - In his transcriptions from 1467MS, Skene misread the words, *Donnchaidh mhic sa barain Donnsleibe* ('Duncan of this son of Baron Donnsléibhe'—see Ronald Black '1467 MS. The MacEwens', *West Highland Notes & Queries*, Ser.3 no.24, Jan 2014, p15-22) to include a son of Dunsleve named 'Sabarain' which he Anglicised first to Savarin (*Collecteana*, 1847) and later to Saveran (*Celtic Scotland*, 1880). The name Saveran occurs nowhere else in Gaelic, and it is undoubtedly from Skene's error that the name Severan is taken. How he comes to be interpreted as son of 'MacEwen' is beyond speculation.

The names of the third and fourth chiefs are lost. - This is consistent with Skene's interpretation of 1467MS in *Celtic Scotland*, and it is only very recently that Ronald Black has been able to read the defective sections of the manuscript (Ronald Black '1467 MS. The MacEwens', *West Highland Notes & Queries*, Ser.3 no.24, Jan 2014, p15-22). From this point, the names of the next four chiefs are as they appear in 1467MS.

Sufnee or Swene, the IX. and last of the Otter chiefs - Swene does not appear in the genealogy of 1467MS which was composed in about the year 1400 during the chiefship of Walter, but he is known from other sources. However, Walter was directly succeeded not by Swene, but by his son Ewen, who appears as witness to a charter of 29 November 1410 (*Highland Papers*, ed. J.R.N. Macphail, 4 vols (Scottish History Society: Edinburgh 1914-34) iv, 233-6; cf. Martin MacGregor, 2000, 'Genealogies of the clans: contributions to the study of MS 1467', *Innes Review*, 51(2), p.131-46).

In place of the list of chiefs given by R. S. T. MacEwen, it is now possible to compile a new list of chiefs based on our better understanding of the extant sources:

        Ewen I (Eoghan)
        Archibald II (Gilleasbaig, *v*.1292-1315)
        Ewen III (Eoghan)
        John IV (Eoin, *v*.1355)
        Walter V (Bhaltair)
        Ewen VI (Eoghan, *v*.1410)
        Swene VII (Suibhne, *v*.1432)

Whereas Swene was undoubtedly the last chief to hold the Barony of Otter, there is no reason to imagine he would have been the last chief of the clan and, although he apparently died without a legitimate son, charters of 1414, 1431 and 1447 reveal male relatives who would have been potential successors to the chiefship according to tanistry (*Argyll Transcripts*). From traditional accounts, it seems the chiefship probably continued after relocation from Otter (see notes "under a chieftain of their own", "in the fifteenth century" below, p12).

"On a rocky point ..." - This reference to the ruins of the medieval *Caisteall Mhic Eoghain* draws on the work of Rev. Alexander MacFarlane in his *Statistical Account of the parish of Kilfinnan*, 1794. R. S. T. MacEwen seemingly encountered this information in the work of W. F. Skene.

In 1431-32 - Here, R. S. T. MacEwen is closely following the entry for 'Kilfinan' in *Origines Parochiales Scotiae*, Vol.II pt.i, p54. The original agreements are preserved in the Campbell archives (see *Argyll Transcripts*, 20th March 1432, 7th June 1432; see also *Highland Papers* II, 96). It is not possible to fully understand the circumstances of this deal on the basis of available evidence.

in 1493 - Although Celestine Campbell is only confirmed in possession of the Barony of Otter in 1493, he uses the designation 'of Otter' as early as 1466 (*Argyll Transcripts*, 10th April 1466).

Otter." So that after the middle of the fifteenth century the barony and estates of Otter passed and gave title to a branch of the Campbells, and the MacEwens became more than ever "children of the mist."

In consequence of their desperate condition the remnant sought new alliances, as a necessity of the times. Some remained in their own neighbourhood and joined the Campbells. In 1602 proof is allowed to Colquhoun of Luss to show that a number of MacGregors, MacLachlans, MacEwens, and MacNeills were "men" of the Earl of Argyll, and that the Earl was answerable for certain depredations committed by them and specified in the complaint. Others joined MacDougal Campbell of Craignish in Lorne. Some of the latter are said to have settled in Lochaber. Besides those who joined the Campbells, some, no doubt, allied themselves to other western clans, for the name was common at one time in the Western Highlands and Islands, especially in Skye. Other colonies were formed in the Lennox country, in Dumbartonshire and in Galloway, while the name is common in Lochaber in connection with the Camerons. This sept was known locally as the "Sliochd-Eoghain." The Muckly family—said to be decended from the Lorne-Macdougal branch—and other families, and many bearing the name still in Argyll and the Isles, are descendants of the old clansmen.*

III.—MacEwens as Bard-Seanachies.

To the men of Otter, broken up as a clan, and bereft of chieftain and lands, the protection of a power-

---

*As an instance of the complete dispersion of the clan, Mr. H. W. Ewen writes that his family have been settled in South Lincolnshire since 1500.

"children of the mist." - The term 'Children of the Mist' usually designates the Clan Gregor after its brutal suppression in 1604. There is no particular reason to believe that Clan Ewen of Otter was in any such 'desperate condition' at this point. Although the loss of the Barony of Otter was certainly a most unwelcome step down the feudal ladder, a chief's authority was ultimately not dependent on his feudal status but on his accepted position at the head of his family—in 1590, it seems that the chiefs of clans Cameron, MacGregor and MacNab were all landless, but still wielded authority over their followers (T. C. Smout, 1969, *A History of the Scottish People*, p41).

joined the Campbells - Relations between Campbells and Clan Ewen seem to have been co-operative or even friendly, and remained so after the Barony of Otter passed into Campbell hands. Although descendants of this Clan Ewen frequently supported Clan Campbell, they appear to have retained their status as an independent clan (see below, p12) and the MacEwen sept within Clan Campbell has another unrelated origin (see below, p8).

In 1602 proof is allowed to Colquhoun of Luss ... - This document of 25 November 1602, which lists twenty seven MacGregor clansmen, forms part of the build up to the Battle of Glen Fruin and the ultimate proscription of Clan Gregor. Among those listed are the sons of Ewen MacGregor of Fearnan, who appear as Gregor McEwen in Moirinsche, John Dow McEwen, and Duncan McEwen. The paternal grandfather of these men was Alasdair Roy MacGregor of Glenstrae, Chief of Clan Gregor, and the patronymic 'McEwen' indicates simply that their father was called Ewen. Another two 'McEwens' who appear near the end of the list are harder to identify, but there is no reason to doubt that they are also MacGregor clansmen. As such, these McEwens are not relevant to a study of Clan Ewen of Otter or any other MacEwen clan. See Amelia Georgiana Murray MacGregor of MacGregor, 1898, *History of the Clan Gregor from Public Records and Private Collections*, Vol.I (AD 878 -1625), p277.

Others joined ... - Here, R. S. T. MacEwen asserts his theory that MacEwens across Scotland are all descended from Clan Ewen of Otter, but he offers no evidence to support his assertion. Although the use of the phrase 'it is said' may seem to suggest oral traditions stretching back centuries, in fact MacEwen laments the paucity of oral traditions (p41), and he always declares his sources when he does make use of them. Instead, these comments relate to scholarly speculation by earlier historians, specifically Keltie (II, p247-8), whose description of the fragmentation of Siol Gillevray in the thirteenth century was mistakenly interpreted by MacEwen to suggest the break-up of Clan Ewen of Otter in the fifteenth century (see note "On the conquest of Argyll by Alexander II." above, p5).

MacDougal Campbell of Craignish - As descendants of Dougal Maul Campbell of Craignish (1156-1190), this branch of Clan Campbell is known in Gaelic as *Mac Dùbhghaill Creaginnis* ('MacDougall of Craignish'). An alternative theory of their origin considers this clan to be descended from a postulated Clan MacEacharn. Whatever the case, despite sharing the MacDougall name, they are not related to the MacDougalls of Clan Dougall.

Mr. H. W. Ewen - Whilst some families, such as the Ewings of Norfolk, may have gone to England with the unification of the English and Scottish crowns under King James VI & I, the English surname Ewen cannot always be assumed to denote Scottish ancestry.

ful chief became a desperate necessity. No doubt the majority of them existed in other clans as fighting auxiliaries, but there is evidence that a few of them found more peaceful occupations. The position of bard and seanachie was an honourable one, and the dispossessed clansmen who obtained these posts suffered no diminution of rank.

Mr. Lovat Fraser in his *Highland Chief** says the MacEwens became hereditary bards of the Campbells; and from old chronicles it appears there were other MacEwen poets and bards in different parts of the country. One lived in Inverness-shire.

The Bard-Seanachies were important functionaries and officers in the Celtic system, and the most learned men in the clan. Originally, in the Druidical period, they were of the priestly and second order of Druids, and in later times they held a high place in the Highland clans, down to the beginning of the eighteenth century. They combined, in their own persons, the offices of Poet-Laureate, Genealogist, and Herald of Arms. They were educated in the science of genealogy, and their work was preserved in the form of rhymes. These they recited on important occasions; just as a Herald of the College of Arms, in the present day, recites the titles of distinguished persons at great public functions. The office was hereditary. Logan says of them: " The Celtic bards were members of the priesthood, and no class of society among the ancients have been more celebrated. . . . Whether we consider the influence which they possessed, their learning or poetic genius, they are one of the most interesting orders of antiquity, and worthy of our entire admiration. . . . Their compositions commemorating the worth and

* *The Celtic Monthly.*

a desperate necessity - In this paragraph, R. S. T. MacEwen assumes that the family of Clan Ewen of Otter fell apart when they lost control of the barony, but there is no evidence to support this opinion. If they had indeed broken up and attached themselves to other clans, they would presumably have also swapped the name MacEwen for clan names appropriate to their new affiliations, so that there would no longer be any trace of them.

Mr. Lovat Fraser - *The Celtic Monthly: A Magazine for Highlanders*, Vol.V, 1897, p74.

hereditary bards - This celebrated family of MacEwens apparently takes its name from one Ewen McDuncan who was acknowledged as a bard in the sixteenth century. They are not connected with Clan Ewen of Otter and are usually regarded as a sept of either Clan Campbell or Clan MacDougall (see for instance, Alasdair Campbell of Airds, 2000, *A History of Clan Campbell*, Vol.I, p7). In *The Companion to Gaelic Scotland* (ed. Derick S. Thomson, Basil Blackwell, 1983) Derick Thomson writes of these McEwen bards: 'They are designated as a bardic family in 1558, when Colin Campbell of Glenorchy granted a charter to Eugenius McDuncane McCarne and to his son Arnaldus or Arnoldus and his heirs male after him who act as *Joculatores* ('wlgariter Rymouris') giving them the two merklands of Barmullocht in the lordship of Lorne.' In 1588, caution was issued in £1,000 by Allan MacDougall of Raray for 'Arne Mckewin of Kilquhair' and others including 'Dougall Mcewin of Barnabuk' and 'Johnne Mcewin Cherverreth' (*Register of the Privy Council*, Vol.IV, p266).

Logan says ... - James Logan, 1831, *The Scotish Gaël*, Vol.II, p212-9. R. S. T. MacEwen's quotations from Logan on the role of bards in Celtic society continue until p10. Logan would no longer be considered a completely reliable source, but his history was groundbreaking in its day.

exploits of heroes were a sort of national annals, which served the double purpose of preserving the memory of past transactions, and of stimulating the youth to an imitation of their virtuous ancestors." They accompanied the clans to war, animating them by the chanting of heroic poems, while each great chief was constantly attended by a number who entertained him at his meals, and roused his own and his followers' courage by powerful recitations. "They also officiated as a sort of aides-de-camp to the chief, communicating his orders to the chieftains and their followers." "An important part of their duty was the preservation of the genealogies and descent of the chiefs and the clan, which were solemnly repeated at marriages, baptisms, and burials. The last purpose for which they were retained by the Highlanders was to preserve a faithful history of their respective clans. . . . From their antiquarian knowledge the bards were called 'Seanachaidh,' from 'Sean,' old, a title synonymous with the Welsh 'Arvydd Vardd,' an officer who latterly was of national appointment, and whose heraldic duties were recognised by the English College of Arms. They attended at the birth, marriage, and death of all persons of high descent, and the marwnod, or elegy, which they composed on the latter occasion, 'was required to contain truly, and at length, the genealogy and descent of the deceased from eight immediate ancestors; to notice the several collateral branches of the family, and to commemorate the surviving wife or husband. These he registered in his books, and delivered a true copy of them to the heir, etc., which was produced the day of the funeral, when all the principal branches of the family and their friends were assembled together in the great hall of the

From their antiquarian knowledge the bards were called 'Seanachaidh' - The Gaelic word *seanchaidh* is literally 'a tradition-bearer' (from *seanchas*, 'old lore').

mansion, and then recited with an audible voice. He also made a visitation called the Bard's Circuit, once every three years, to all the gentlemen's houses, where he registered and corrected their armorial bearings. . . . Some of their awards of arms are of as late a date as 1703. The Bard had a stipend paid out of every plough land, and the chief was called 'King of the Bards.'" *

Dr. Johnson's sceptical spirit refused to be satisfied with the popular accounts of the bards and seanachies. He professed to have made searching enquiries into their early history with very unsatisfactory results. "Neither bards nor senachies," he says, "could write or read."—*(Journey to the Western Islands.)* For this daring calumny he has been brought to task by his critics. The Rev. Donald MacNicol in his *Remarks on Dr. Samuel Johnson's Journey to the Highlands* (1779), has some interesting remarks on the matter. He tells us that "the MacEwens had free lands in Lorn in Argyleshire, for acting as bards to the family of Argyll, to that of Breadalbane, and likewise to Sir John Macdougall of Dunolly, in 1572. The two last of the race were Aime and his son Neil. I have now before me an elegy upon the death of Sir Duncan Dow Campbell of Glenurchy, composed by Neil MacEwen. The date, which is 1630, is in the body of the poem. How long he lived after this I cannot take upon me to say, but as there is much of the history and genealogy of the family interwoven with the performance, he must certainly have been both bard and sennachie." And further on in the same book, he says, referring to Irish Gaelic: "We have a striking instance of this in the

* *The Scottish Gael*, Vol. ii.

Rev. Donald MacNicol - Donald MacNicol, 1779, *Remarks on Dr. Samuel Johnson's Journey to the Hebrides*, p245-6.

Aime - this should read 'Airne' (as it does in MacNicol's original) for Gaelic, *Athairne*. Alexander Campbell, author of 'The Manuscript History of Craignish' (c.1719-1725) writes that Neil MacEwen was the last of his line, and that he died in around 1650.

further on - Donald MacNicol, 1779, *Remarks on Dr. Samuel Johnson's Journey to the Hebrides*, p269-70.

elegy of Sir Duncan Dow Campbell . . . composed by the bard, Neil MacEwen, in 1630. This poem is in many places altogether unintelligible to most Highlanders, though other productions of a much earlier date, as being composed in the *Albion* dialectic of the Celtic, are perfectly understood. . . . But MacEwen was one of those bards who resided sometimes in Ireland. His poem is in the Gaelic character, and in his own handwriting; and it is still preserved among the papers of the family of Breadalbane at Taymouth."

Mr. J. F. Campbell, in his *Tales of the West Highlands*, furnishes an example of the work of one of the MacEwen bard-seanachies from a MS. which came from Cawdor Castle, and which contains the following preamble: "Genealogy Abridgement of the Very Ancient and Notable Family of Argyll, 1779"; wherein the writer explains that "In the following account we have had regard to the genealogical tree done by Neil MacEwen, as he received the same from Eachern MacEwen, his father, as he had the same from Arthur MacEwen, his grandfather, and their ancestors and predecessors, senachies and pensioners to great families, who for many ages were employed to make up and keep such records in their accustomed way of Irish rhymes."

IV.—THE LENNOX SEPT.
MACEWENS, EWENS, EWINGS, ETC.

A considerable sept of the clan settled early in Dumbartonshire, on the shores of Loch Lomond, and in the Lennox country, owning allegiance to the Stewart Earls of Lennox, who were descended from Bancho, Thane of Lochaber, the ancestor of the Royal line. As early as the tenth century the Scots occupied

MacEwen was one of those - The MacEwen bards were classical Gaelic poets and their language was a literary language close to that of the classical Gaelic poets of Ireland. Their frequent use of the name Arne (Gaelic, *Athairne*) has led to the suggestion that they might be a branch of the Irish bardic family of O'Hosey (Gaelic, *O hEoghusa*; see Campbell of Airds, p7).

an example of the work - This reference to MacEwen's genealogy of the Campbells appears in John Francis Campbell's *Popular Tales of the West Highlands* (Vol.2, 1860-1, p94) because it traces the Campbell line through the legendary Diarmaid.
Neil MacEwen's genealogy of the Campbells is preserved in the National Archives of Scotland, Edinburgh (NAS GD/112/57/8/21) under the Latin title, *Epitome vere prosapie inclyte celeberrime ac antiquissime gentis Cambellorum ut Nigellus MacKewnius Fernoche in Melphortia cuippie fide digno tradidit, hanc etiam se ex antiquis veterum scriptis summa qua potuit diligentia, fide ac studio collegisse asseruit ac sic exorsus est.*

THE LENNOX SEPT - The term 'sept' is usually used to denote a sub-division of a clan and indeed, as R. S. T. MacEwen mistakenly regarded all these separate families as branches of a single clan, this may well be the intended sense here.

Strath-Clyde, and Gaelic was the language from Renfrew to Galloway for several centuries. It has left its impress still strong in personal and place names in that region.* It is not astonishing therefore that Argyleshire Scots should at a later date migrate to the shores of the Clyde and to Galloway. Gaelic in time disappeared before the inroads of the Teutonic language in the districts bordering on the Highland line as it had done in the southern districts at an earlier period. The people in a few generations lost touch with the Highlands; they no longer spoke Gaelic, they were incorporated with the southern inhabitants, and in character and sentiment they became a Lowland people, although originally of pure Celtic descent.

The Lennox sept received grants of land in the district to which they gave their name. Between 1625 and 1680 there are at least four charters in which successive Dukes of Lennox and Richmond are served heirs in the lands of "MacKewin" and "McEwin," as the name was then written.† But there is reason to believe their advent there was much earlier. According to tradition, this sept, under a chieftain of their own, sought the protection of Levenach, the Celtic Earl, in the fifteenth century. They are said to have joined the standard of Mary, under Lennox, and to have fought at Langside in 1568, where they received a banner which seems to have gone the way of many other ancient clan banners. They were a powerful race of men and a story used to be told in connection with an old stone coffin which at one time lay in the MacEwen burying-ground, that a man of

* Dr. Macbain in *The Transactions of the Inverness Gaelic Society*, Vol. xxi.

† Report on the Public Records of Scotland.

Gaelic in time disappeared - Gaelic was apparently spoken in Luss, Dumbartonshire, as late as the nineteenth century (John Stoddart, 1801, *Remarks on local scenery & manners in Scotland during the years 1799 and 1800*, vol.I, p228). Dorothy Wordsworth noted that the innkeeper in Tarbet had difficulty understanding English when she and William visited in 1803 (Wordsworth, *Recollections of a Tour Made in Scotland*, 1997, p90). Similarly, the 'Highland Girl' of William Wordsworth's poem, who they met at Inversnaid, Stirling, had 'few words of English speech.'

the lands of "MacKewin" and "McEwin" - The locality described here as the 'lands' of MacEwen is the farmstead of Wester Glenboig, near Fintry, on the border between Stirling and Dumbarton. This farm within the earldom of Lennox was occupied by a family sometimes known as MacEwen. The earliest reference to this family is a charter of 1522/3 by John, Earl of Lennox, to Donald Nenbog son and heir of Patrik Nenbog of the lands of Wester Glenbog—the use of the name MacEwen for either farm or family is first recorded in 1614 (NAS GD1/393/47). The four charters cited by R. S. T. MacEwen appear in *Inquisitionem ad Capellam Domini Regis Retornatarum*, and refer to two separate Glenboig estates, Glenboig-Cunningham and Glenboig-Macewin. According to the charter of 1614 and a legal judgement of 22 June 1802 Wester Glenboig comprised five merkland (NAS GD1/393/47 and 'Davidson against Hill' in *The Decisions of the Court of Session*). According to John Guthrie Smith, Glenboig-Macewin is to be identified with Wester Glenboig, and Glenboig-Cunningham with Middle Glenboig (see note "Mr. Guthrie Smith" below, p13).

According to tradition - R. S. T. MacEwen's most important source for this clan is undoubtedly the letter of 1885 referred to on the next page (p13), but as a descendant of Walter MacEwen in Luss, he may himself have known some of these traditions from his early years. Without the work of R. S. T. MacEwen, these traditions would undoubtedly have been lost.

under a chieftain of their own - If this clan is identical with Clan Ewen of Otter, as seems more-or-less beyond doubt, this tradition confirms that the line of chiefs did not stop with the death of Swene, lord of Otter, but that he was succeeded by a new chief whose name is not recorded here (see note "Sufnee or Swene, the IX. and last of the Otter chiefs" above, p6). MacEwen interprets this tradition according to his own belief that this represents only a small sept of a much larger clan, but careful distinctions between terms such as 'sept' and 'clan' or 'chief and chieftain' are Victorian innovations, and it is difficult to see how they could have formed part of the original oral tradition.

in the fifteenth century - As we will see below (see notes "in the middle of the fifteenth century" below, p14, and "Early in the eighteenth century" below, p16) chronology is not always a strength of oral tradition. However, this date roughly corresponds with the first appearance of the surnames or clan names (as opposed to patronymics) Ewing and MacEwen in this area, and also tallies with the known dates for the loss of the Barony of Otter.

under Lennox - In 1568, Lennox supported his grandson the young King James VI but did not take part in the battle, so the clan would have mustered under the command of Archibald Campbell, Earl of Argyll, which suggests the clan was loyal either to Argyll or to the queen. According to Jim Finegan (1995, *History and Legends of Clan MacLachlan*, p36) a William Ewing served at Langside as a flag bearer for the queen.

where they received a banner - A new clan banner is dependent on a new grant of arms. The Forman Workman MS or Workman Armorial in Lyon Office records a shield in the Ewing name which may have been granted in 1566 (see note "Keppoch" below, p43), and this would undoubtedly have led the clan to muster under a new banner in 1568. If William Ewing was a flag bearer for Mary Queen of Scots (see note "under Lennox" above) his appointment would seem to have been memorialised in the ensignment of the Ewing shield—the combination of his new role as flag bearer with his own new banner will have made William Ewing's appearance at Langside especially memorable for the clan.

a story used to be told - No other source is cited for this local Luss tradition, and it seems most likely that R. S. T. MacEwen heard the story of this stone coffin from his father.

the clan carried the coffin under one arm, and the lid under the other, from the loch to the churchyard of Luss. A descendant of one of these families, who died in 1898 at the age of seventy-eight, writing in 1885, after referring to these traditions, said: "These MacEwens certainly belonged to Dumbartonshire, on Loch Lomond, and had been there for many generations. The name in olden times was spelt with the *a*—McEwan—and there was a paper in the family tracing them back to the Battle of Langside, where they won their colours (the standard referred to) fighting for Queen Mary. All the old tombstones not claimed by families living in the parish were destroyed years ago, so there is no memorial left of this branch of the old MacEwen race."

Mr. Guthrie Smith, in his *History of Strathendrick*, has the following account of the Glenboig family: "In 1614 there was a charter granted by the Duke of Lennox to William Neaubog, *alias* Macewin, eldest son and heir of William Mackewin, *alias* Neaubog de Glenbog Wester. In 1691 the proprietor was James McAine, called in 1698 James Macewan. In the Valuation Roll of 1723 the following appears : 'John Williamson and Janet Ure, his spouse, their equal share of the five-merk lands of Wester Glenboig, £46 14s. 4d.; John Buchanan, maltman, and Jane Ure, his spouse, their equal half of the five-merk lands of Wester Glenboig, £46 14s. 4d.' These Williamsons (if the first Williamson was not himself a William MacEwan who changed his name after the fashion of the time) appear to have succeeded the Macewans of Glenboig. The greater part of the lands of Wester Glenboig was afterwards acquired by Napier of

the MacEwen burying-ground ... the churchyard of Luss - R. S. T. MacEwen's direct paternal ancestors were from Luss, Dumbartonshire (now Argyll & Bute), but he was born in Evelix, Sutherland, so he no doubt considered Luss as the old family burying ground. There is no reason to imagine that Ewings or McEwans from other places were ever buried there.

A descendant of one of these families - This description would of course include R. S. T. MacEwen himself, but the other details suggest that his correspondent might have been Archibald McEwen, who appears in the 1891 census for Luss aged seventy-one and gives his birthplace as Dumbartonshire.

a paper in the family - This paper probably recorded traditions which had been preserved orally over a number of generations and traced the McEwan family of Luss back to their sixteenth century ancestors, who seem to have 'belonged to Dumbartonshire, on Loch Lomond' although not necessarily to Luss. The spelling 'McEwan' apparently used in the paper need not be assumed to have had any greater antiquity than the paper itself. MacEwen's correspondent refers to the tradition (cited above, p12) that they fought for Queen Mary at Langside under a new banner. He imagines they won this banner through their bravery in battle, but this is not consistent with the circumstances of the battle.

the standard referred to - More information about this standard or banner was presumably included in the original letter, underlining its significance in clan tradition.

there is no memorial - Whereas the MacEwen name is recorded in seventeenth-century parish records for Dumbartonshire, the Ewing name is very much more common—for instance, in early registers (before 1700) for the county, there are 76 Ewing births compared with just 8 MacEwens. Thus in Dumbartonshire, the standard Scots or English form of Gaelic *Mac Eoghain* was clearly 'Ewing' or 'Euing'. However, although too early to be the great grandfather of R. S. T. MacEwen (b.1839), it is interesting that a Walter Mckewn son of John Mckewn was baptised in Luss in 1698, and he probably represents the same family line; that this family preserved clan traditions relating to the Ewing name may confirm the continuing use of the *Mac Eoghain* form in spoken Gaelic long after the written form 'Ewing' had become widespread. Although one or two families may have adopted another form of the name, with relatively few exceptions, the descendants of this clan will be known today by the surname Ewing.

Mr. Guthrie Smith - John Guthrie Smith, 1896, *Strathendrick, and its inhabitants from early times*, p243. It has not been possible to discover whether the now extinct family of the McEwans of Wester Glenboig were a part of the same clan as the Ewings of Dumbartonshire, but their proximity to later Ewing houses at Craigtoun, Ballikinrain and Cardross House certainly raises that possibility.

Ballikinrain. But in 1796 there was a William MacEwan of Glenboig, writer in Edinburgh, who received a grant of arms at that date from the Lyon office. Netherton, the other division of the estate, is (1890) farmed by Mr. James Ewing (another form of the name), who belongs to a family who have long been tenants there."

There are numerous families and persons bearing the clan name at the present day in Dumbarton, Stirling,* Clackmannan, Renfrew, Lanark, Ayr, on the banks of the Clyde, and in the surrounding districts. Mr. William McEwan, late M.P. for Central Edinburgh, the magnificent donor of the "McEwan Hall," belongs to a Clackmannan family. There have been in the past, and there are now, several Ewen and Ewing families of position and affluence in the Lennox country and the surrounding districts—the Ewens or Ewings of Craigtown and Keppock, of Glasgow, Levenfield, Ballikinrain, &c.

V.—MacEwens in Galloway.

According to tradition, this branch of the clan made its appearance in Galloway at an early period— in the middle of the fifteenth century,—about the time of the dispersion from Otter. A descendant † of the family of High Mark, Wigtonshire, furnishes the following interesting account of the sept:—

"The late Sir Andrew Agnew, in his history of *The Agnews in Galloway,* states that about the middle of the fifteenth century the Laird of Lochnaw was

---

* The Stirlingshire branch is of considerable antiquity. Mr. R. MacEwen, Clifton, informs us that in his family burying-ground in St. Ninian's Churchyard, Stirling, a stone bears the date of 1614.

† Mr. John McEwen, Girvan, Ayrshire.

William MacEwan of Glenboig - Despite the remarkable coincidence of names, William Macewan has no connection with Wester Glenboig, near Fintry, Stirling, but takes his designation from Glenboig in Lanarkshire. His nephew and heir, John Carfrae of Glenboig (cf. NAS CS34/7/130) is listed among Justices of the Peace for Lanarkshire and voted in the Lanarkshire constituency in the General Election of 1818. From his grant of arms in 1796, it is clear that William Macewan was in fact a Cameron (see notes below, "Macewan of Glenboig" p35, "Glenboig, County of Stirling" p44, "Glenboig (Stirling)" p45).

Netherton - Netherton and Overton together make up Easter Glenboig, also known as 'Glenboig Cunningham'.

Mr. William McEwan - This is the brewer William McEwan (1827-1913) who was Liberal M.P. for Edinburgh Central from 1886 until 1900.

several Ewen and Ewing families - Even as late as the nineteenth century, the two names are not always clearly distinguished. As a general rule, the Ewing form is distinctive of the west where 'Ewen' was only an occasional variant, while the forms Ewen, Ewan and Ewans are typical of the eastern Lowlands. Although there is confusion between these names, there does appear to be a Lowland family local to eastern Scotland which is distinct from the (originally Highland) Ewings of western Scotland.

in the middle of the fifteenth century - This dating is unsafe, see notes "the late Sir Andrew Agnew" below, and "the Black Douglas" below, p15. Mr. John McEwen describes the castle as it existed until 1390, but has confused the attack of that year with a later attack on its successor castle in 1451. No doubt, this confusion has arisen from an attempt to reconcile oral traditions of the Galloway McEwens with written histories focussing on Clan Ewen of Otter.

The late Sir Andrew Agnew - Sir Andrew Agnew of Lochnaw, 8th Baronet (1818-92). Agnew's account of this incident is told in his book, *The Hereditary Sheriffs of Galloway*, 1864 (1893), p234-5. Although he seems to defer completely to Sir Andrew's written account, Mr. John McEwen actually records a variant of the story and may have known it directly from oral tradition.

Girvan, Ayrshire - Links between Galloway and Carrick (now part of Ayrshire) are well-established and long-standing. This family connection between Galloway and Girvan is just one instance of contact between the two regions (for another example, see note "Baor" below, p15).

besieged in his castle, which was then situated on the island in the middle of the loch, by the retainers of the Black Douglas, with whom the Agnews had a feud regarding the Sheriffdom of Galloway. When the besieged were on the point of capitulation they were surprised to see, one day, that their enemies had been attacked in the rear by another armed force, and they sallied out, and with the aid of their new allies routed the forces of the Douglas. To recompense these allies—who were the remnant of a broken Highland clan called M°Ewen—the Laird of Lochnaw gave them the tenantship of four of his farms—Knock, Maize, Achnoterach, and High Mark—and their descendants are in occupation of the two latter to the present day.

"In a private letter to Mr. Robert M°Ewen, R.N., in 1840, Sir Andrew Agnew, while recommending him to the Lords of the Admirality for a commission, states that he could recommend him not only because he knew him personally, but also from the fact that 'his family had been tenants on his estates from time immemorial.'

"One of the family (a Covenanter) was shot by command of Claverhouse at the village of Baor, in Ayrshire, and was buried, and a headstone was erected to his memory in the churchyard there. Another of the family at this time was ruling elder of the Parish Church of Leswaet, and through him the old church Bible which Richard Cameron (the Cameronian leader) had used and preached from, came into the possession of the family, and is now in that of the writer.

"Early in the eighteenth century another of the family, Andrew M°Kewan, was killed by command of the Earl of Cassils, for although

the Black Douglas - 'Black Douglas' can denote any of the Earls of Douglas, but this must refer to Black Archibald Douglas (d.1400), who was appointed Sheriff of Galloway in 1369 and who sacked Lochnaw Castle in 1390, since when the original castle has remained a ruin in the loch. Sir Andrew Agnew is clear (*The Hereditary Sheriffs*, p233-5) that Black Archibald was the antagonist and that the Agnews later sought redress at the court of King Robert III (1390-1406). The Agnews were restored to Lochnaw in 1426 and hostilities resumed with the Douglasses in 1451, but the castle of Lochnaw was then very different from that described in Mr. McEwen's account. This means the whole incident must have occurred in 1390, well before any possible 'dispersion' of Clan Ewen of Otter. Their presence in fourteenth-century Galloway at a time when Clan Ewen of Otter was still firmly established in Argyll shows that McEwens in Galloway are a separate clan with their own history and traditions. The Agnews had been Lords of Larne in Ulster since the twelfth century, where they were allied with the McKeown Bissets of Glenarm. According to Agnew's *Hereditary Sheriffs*, they reached Galloway in 1330 to become Constables of Lochnaw. It would appear that a branch of the McKeowns of Glenarm must have accompanied the Agnews to Scotland, where their name was rendered as McEwen. This interpretation is consistent with the appearance in 1331 of Patrick McEwyn as Provost of Wigtown and, crucially, it explains the heraldic crest and motto of the Galloway McEwens (see note "Reviresco" below, p18).

a broken Highland clan - Both Mr. John McEwen and Sir Andrew Agnew must have known of Clan Ewen of Otter from their reading, and have apparently re-interpreted their own traditions in the light of this knowledge. It is however not possible to reconcile the tradition of the McEwens springing to the aid of the Agnews with the notion that they were wandering 'broken' Highland clansmen (see note "The Black Douglas" above). Aside from any arguments based on particular historical evidence, the scenario portrayed here is simply so unlikely as to be literally incredible.

Knock, Maize, Achnoterach, and High Mark - Knock and Maize are near Portslogan, Auchnotteroch near Glaik, and High Mark near Galdenoch, all in the Rhins of Galloway.

Mr. Robert McEwen, R.N. - Robert McEwen (1808-1860), Chief Engineer, H.M.S. Curacoa, see p17.

from time immemorial - This comment by Sir Andrew Agnew, 7th Baronet (1793-1849), father of the author of *The Hereditary Sheriffs*, seems to contradict any suggestion that the McEwens had arrived in Galloway at a specific date remembered in local lore.

Baor - Barr, near Girvan, Ayrshire. The gravestone names the victim as Edward McKeen, shot in 1685 'for adherence to the Word of God and Scotland's Covenanted work of Reformation.' Edward McKeen's surname appears as Kyan, Mackeen, McKean, McKeane, McKian, McCean and McKen (see note "McKeown" below, p17). According to Woodrow's *History of the Sufferings of the Church of Scotland*, Vol.IV, p241, he was 'a pious good man from Galloway, lately come thence to buy corn ... He was asked where he lived, and told them, upon the water of Menock.'

Leswaet - Leswalt, Rhins of Galloway, is about 1½ miles from Lochnaw Castle.

Claverhouse - Sir John Graham of Claverhouse, Viscount Dundee (1648-89), known to his supporters as 'Bonnie Dundee' and to his enemies as 'Bloody Clavers', waged war against the Covenanters on behalf of King Charles II. This period has become known as The Killing Time.

Richard Cameron - Richard Cameron (1648-80) was a Covenanter leader. Ordained minister in summer 1679, he revived the Covenanter cause on 22nd June 1680 when, accompanied by 20 armed men, his brother Michael read out a Declaration, denying the right of government to control religion and denouncing King Charles II as a tyrant. On 22nd July, he was killed in a battle with government dragoons at Airds Moss. His followers, the Cameronians, later formed the core of a regiment of the same name in the British army.

the Earl of Cassils - Cassillis, near Maybole, Ayrshire, was home to the Kennedys from the late thirteenth century and, in 1502, David, Lord Kennedy, was appointed Earl of Cassilis, a title which his successors held until 1831 when the 12th Earl was created Marquess of Ailsa. The Earls of Cassilis wielded such power over South West Scotland in the sixteenth and early seventeenth centuries that they were known as the 'Kings of Carrick'.

> Frae Wigtown tae the town o' Ayr,
> Portpatrick tae the Cruines o' Cree,
> Nae man can get a binding there
> Unless he court St. Kennedie.

McKewan was too independent to give up his farm to a follower of Kennedy at the latter's request, and met his death as the result. When tried for the crime, Kennedy was ordered to pay the widow of McKewan a large quantity of cattle to recompense her for the death of her husband. So much for the law and justice, and the value set on men's lives in those days.

"At the time of the rebellion of the '45 Sir Andrew Agnew took the field for King George, accompanied by two dhuin vassals, John and Thomas McEwen from High Mark; while two other brothers, Robert and Gideon, took the Jacobite side and followed the fortunes of Prince Charles. The story goes that when Sir Andrew Agnew was besieged in Blair Castle, going the rounds one day he passed John McEwen, and in looking out at the rebel forces he also saw the brother Robert, the Jacobite. Turning to John he said, 'Jock, do you see Rab?' and on being answered in the affirmative, he ordered him to 'Shoot the beggar,' a command which, it is needless to say, was not carried out, for after all 'blood is thicker than water.' This John McEwen afterwards went to the Continent with Sir Andrew Agnew, and was present at the Battle of Dettingen, where Sir Andrew commanded the North British Fusiliers.

"The grandson of John McEwen, born in 1766, and also John by name, ran away to sea when in his teens, and during his first voyage was pressed into the Royal Navy, and for seven years was in active service. When he received his discharge he sailed as

Frae Wigtown - Mr John McEwen is a unique source for this version of the rhyme, better known from *The New Statistical Account of Scotland*, (Blackwood, 1845) Vol.IV p88. It is first recorded by Andrew Symson in *A Large Description of Galloway*, 1684 (Edinb. 1823); other versions are in Rev. William Abercrombie's *A Description of Carrict*, 1683-1722, (Scot. Hist. Soc. Edin., 1907) and *Galloway and the Covenanters; or, The struggle for religious liberty in the south-west of Scotland* (Alexander S. Morton, 1914, Gardner, Paisley).

Early in the eighteenth century - This event actually occurred at the start of the seventeenth century. McKewan was the victim of a quarrel between John, 5th Earl of Cassilis, and his brother Hugh, who wanted to let McKewan's farm to his own man. Details are recorded in the *Historie of the Kennedyis* (Robert Pitcairn, *Historical and Genealogical Account of the Principal Families of the Name of Kennedy*, 1830, p28-9). The *Historie* describes McKewan as 'ane prowd carle... heffand Colzeone and the Schereff of Galloway to maynteyne him' ('a proud peasant... having [Sir Thomas Kennedy, lord of] Culzean and the Sheriff of Galloway [Sir Andrew Agnew of Lochnaw] to maintain him'). The slaughter of Andrew McKewan was raised twice at Privy Council, once in 1600 and again in 1601 (*Register of the Privy Council*, Vol. VI, p665, p674).

When tried for the crime - Hugh Kennedy, Master of Cassilis, was granted remission under the Great Seal for the slaughter of 'Andrew McKewan in Auchatroche', 14th September 1601 (*Register of the Great Seal*, xliii 179). The farm of Auchnotteroch is among those listed by Mr. John McEwen above, p15. Although McKewan himself seems to have only recently taken up his lease on the farm at the time of his death, it could have previously been let to his family, and it may be that he was granted this lease in the teeth of opposition from the Master of Cassilis because he was felt to have some traditional right to it. Although the account in the *Historie of the Kennedyis* emphasises Culzean's role in securing the farm for McKewan rather than Lochnaw's, this might have more to do with their relative importance to the main subject of the *Historie*, where McKewan's death is a minor incident in the story of the feud between branches of Clan Kennedy.

the '45 - In 1745, Charles Edward Stuart, the 'Young Pretender' or 'Bonnie Prince Charlie', invaded Scotland with the intention to depose King George II. The Stuart cause had been dubbed 'Jacobite' from 1689, when it pitted the followers of the former king, James (Latin, *Jacobus*) VII & II, against the 'Williamite' supporters of William of Orange. Families with a Covenanter background tended to oppose the Jacobites, who in the aftermath of Scotland's Killing Time were often regarded by them as Catholic tyrants. After the Union of 1707, the Jacobite cause became associated with Scottish independence.

Sir Andrew Agnew - Lieutenant General Sir Andrew Agnew of Lochnaw, 5th Baronet (1687-1771). He was, in the words of Sir Walter Scott, 'a soldier of the old military school, severe in discipline, stiff and formal in manners, brave to the last degree, but somewhat of an humourist' (*Tales of a Grandfather*, Vol.III, 1842, p278). This anecdote is typical of the stories surrounding him.

dhuin vassals - 'gentlemen' (Gaelic, *dhuin'-uasal, dhaoine-uasal*)

Blair Castle - The Siege of Blair Castle began on 17th March 1746. Sir Andrew Agnew ordered his garrison of 270 men not to fire on the besieging Jacobites unless attacked, but refused to surrender the castle. The siege was lifted when a relief force arrived on 2nd April and, two weeks later, Agnew and his men took part in the Battle of Culloden, 16th April 1746.

High Mark - One of the four McEwen farms listed above on p15.

Battle of Dettingen - 27th June 1743. British and Hanoverian forces led by King George II defeated the French army commanded by the Duc de Noailles.

North British Fusiliers - The 21st (Royal North British Fusilier) Regiment of Foot was renamed the Royal Scots Fusiliers in 1877. The custom of referring to Scotland as 'North Britain' began with the accession of King James VI of Scots to the English throne in 1603, but became more common after the Act of Union in 1707. At the Battle of Dettingen the Royal North British Fusiliers destroyed the French Cuirassiers after Lieutenant Colonel Sir Andrew Agnew famously issued the command, 'Dinna fire till ye can see the whites o' their e'en.'

first officer of the privateer 'Mary,' of Liverpool, under Captain Thompson, who was mortally wounded in the first engagement. Before his death he handed the command of the vessel over to McEwen, writing on the back of the Letter of Marque, 'From James Thompson, commander, to John McEwen.' This document, signed by the Lords of the Admiralty in 1793, is now in possession of the writer. After making some prize money in command of the privateer, M'Ewen bought the hull of a Government transport, and after fitting her out sailed with a cargo to the West Indies; but on his return with a cargo of sugar he was wrecked on the north-west coast of Africa, losing all he had on board except his quadrant, now in the possession of his great-grandson.

"Captain McEwen left a son, Robert, who became a marine engineer and was the first to erect a steam engine in Russia, and was presented by the Czar Nicholas with a cup for his services. He was awarded the Isis Gold Medal of the Royal Society of Arts on two occasions: 1st, for his safe mercurial steam guage; and, 2nd, for his machine for hot pressing lace goods. The cup and medals are also in the possession of the writer. He received a commission in the Royal Navy, and died at Monte Video in 1860 on board H.M.S. 'Curacoa.'

"In the old family Bibles, and in the burying-place in Leswaet Churchyard, near Stranraer, the name is spelt in various ways, as McKewan, McKeown, McEwine, McEwing, McEwan, and in later times McEwen, the form now generally adopted.

"On the farm of High Mark, Leswaet, the names of the fields are evidently of Gaelic origin; and there is also a cove on the shore called 'Otter Cove,' pro-

Leswaet - Leswalt, Rhins of Galloway.

McKeown - This is the form most often used by descendants of the *Mac Eoin* Bissets in Ireland, and invariably translates *Mac Eoin* rather than *Mac Eoghain*. The regular use of forms such as McKeown, McKean and Mackeen (see note "Baor" above, p15) as variant forms of the name in Galloway recalls the likely origin of this family as a branch of the *Mac Eoin* Bissets (see notes "the Black Douglas" above, p15, "Reviresco" below, p18).

the names of the fields - Galloway had its own distinctive form of Gaelic which was spoken up until the eighteenth century, and it would be surprising if the place names were not in the native tongue. The placename 'Armakewne' recorded in a charter of 1466 concerning Balmaclellan may represent Gaelic *Earrann Mhic Eoin*, 'the portion of McKeown' (*Register of the Great Seal of Scotland 1424-1513*, Vol. II, no. 907; 'Armakewne' is probably either Ironmacannie or a lost placename very nearby); this placename is recorded too early for a link with any dispersal of Clan Ewen of Otter to seem plausible, especially since it was not in the possession of a MacEwen in 1466.

'Otter Cove' - The Barony of Otter in Argyll takes its name from the Gaelic *an Oitir*, which means a spit of sand or gravel. No 'Otter Cove' is shown on the Ordnance Survey map near the farm of High Mark, but this Otter Cove could have been named in Gaelic after a spit of sand or gravel or, if named in more recent times, it may simply refer to otters living there. Even if there were any evidence that Galloway McEwens might be connected with Clan Ewen of Otter, it would be highly improbable that the name of this cove might be similarly connected.

bably so named after the original home of the race. In the days of the 'Free Traders' it was no doubt a convenient shelter and landing place. A member of the family who got into trouble over his 'trading' is said to have escaped to the Isle of Man, where he was joined by his wife and family, and became the ancestor of a family of the name in that island."

There is an old seal in the family showing an oak tree springing into leaf again, with the motto "Reviresco" over it. It was used by Robert McEwen in his lifetime, but is of much older date.*

There are, besides the writer, other descendants of these Galloway families."

VI.—MacEwens in Lochaber.

Sliochd Eoghain.

Keltie, in his *History of the Highland Clans*, says the original seat of the MacEwens was in Lochaber. This must have been before the thirteenth century, for we find them at Otter, in Cowal, in 1222; when, with other western clans, they suffered severely in the conquest of Argyll by Alexander II. According to the manuscript of 1450, the Siol Gillevray—from whom the MacEwens, MacNeills, and MacLachlans are derived—are descended from a certain Gillebride, King of the Isles, ancestor of the MacDonalds. Skene doubts the Gillebride genealogy, and favours the descent from Anradan and Aodha Alain (De Dalan), as given in chapter ii., "but, nevertheless, the traditionary affinity which is thus shown to have existed between these clans and the race of Somerled at so early a period, he thinks seems to countenance the

* See post on the subject of these family seals.

'Free Traders' - Smugglers. In Scott's 1815 novel, *Guy Mannering*, which is set in Galloway in the late eighteenth century, the aristocratic Mr Bertram speaks of 'free-traders, whom the law calls smugglers'.

Isle of Man - The Isle of Man was a notorious haunt of smugglers.

"Reviresco" - The crest and motto used by the McEwens in Galloway hark back directly to their Bisset ancestry (see note "the Black Douglas" above, p15, and *Fig.8* below, p25). The Bisset crest of a sprouting oak stump is identical with this McEwen crest and, although the official motto of Clan Bisset is '*Abscissa Virescit*', others are also traditional within the clan including '*Revirescit*' and '*Reviresco*' (cf. James Fairbairn, *Crests of the Families of Great Britain and Ireland*). Both crest and motto (in its various forms) were probably adopted by the Bissets following the dramatic expulsion of John Bisset after 1242. It is after this John (or Eoin) that the MacEoin or McKeown Bissets of Glenarm took their name. That the Galloway McEwens share both their crest and motto with the Bissets cannot be merely coincidental, and must be understood as a statement of their distant ancestry, whether as direct descendants of Eoin Bisset himself or of his Irish retinue.

The full story of McEwens, McKeans, McKeowns and McKowns in Galloway may however be more complex than this evidence would suggest. There is a tradition that McCowans and McGowans in Nithsdale are descended from Owen the Bald, King of Strathclyde (Latin, *Eugenius Calvus*, d.1018), and that they served under Robert the Bruce (Hugh Lorimer, 1952, *A Corner of Old Strathclyde*, p100-1; George F. Black, 1946, *The Surnames of Scotland*, p505), but although there is likely to be more than one family here, they are not easily distinguishable by surname—according to Patrick Dudgeon, Galloway makes no distinction between the names 'Owen, McEwen, McKean, McKeoune, McCowan, McGowan, &c., all of which are substantially the same.' (1888, *"Macs" in Galloway*, p23).

Keltie - John Scott Keltie, 1875, *A History of the Scottish Highlands, Highland Clans and Scottish Regiments*. Keltie's remarks relate not to the MacEwens but to the origins of Siol Gillevray, see note "On the conquest of Argyll by Alexander II." above, p5.

notion that they had all originally sprung from the same stock." * The MacNeills were certainly vassals of the Lords of the Isles; and according to Keltie, the Camerons were connected with the House of Islay in the reign of Robert Bruce, and their modern possessions, Lochiel and Locharkaig, belonged to the Lords of the Isles. They are said to have deserted Alexander, Lord of the Isles, for James I. MacKenzie, in his *History of the Camerons*, also says that the MacLachlans of Strath-Lachlan are said to be descended from the Camerons and related to the MacLachlans of Coruanan, "and this may have been the link which led Donald Dubh, the celebrated 'Taillear' Cameron warrior, to Cowal when he tired of a fighting life in Lochaber."†

It is curious that tradition should have associated the *three* Siol Gillevray clans—which are western clans—with the Camerons in Lochaber—which is a Moravian clan—if there was no connection existing between them; and that Donald Dubh should have fled to and settled in Cowal, where the MacEwen and the MacLachlan territories lay, if he was not sure of a kinsman's welcome. Again, the name of Ewen is very common in the Cameron family. It appears as early as 1219, when Sir Ewen de Cambron, third son of the fourth chief, is mentioned in the Chartulary of Arbroath. Up to the close of the fourteenth century the history of the Camerons is meagre and imperfect, and the name does not appear again till we come to Ewen, eldest son of Allan, the ninth chief. This Ewen became tenth chief (1390-96), and was the chief in 1396 in the fight on the North Inch of Perth.

* Keltie, Vol. ii., p. 162.
† *History of the Camerons*, MacKenzie.

MacNeills - Clan MacNeil is traditionally considered part of the Anrothan Kindred (see note "On the conquest of Argyll by Alexander II." above, p5), although recent DNA analysis has shown that, like the descendants of Somerled, their direct agnatic line is in fact Norse.

MacLachlans of Strath-Lachlan - Mackenzie does indeed make this claim (on p54) but must be in error. These two groups of MacLachlans may indeed be related, but the MacLachlans of Strathlachlan are universally accepted as the senior house and their genealogy is found in 1467MS where they are among the Anrothan Kindred (see note "On the conquest of Argyll by Alexander II." above, p5). The MacLachlans of Coruanan are thought to be descended from the MacLachlans of Innischonnell, who were loyal to the Earls of Argyll.

Donald Dubh - Donald McEwen Beg Cameron, known as *an Taillear Dubh* (though not as *Domhnall Dubh* or 'Donald Dow') was one of the protagonists in the Erracht Feud within Clan Cameron (1567-77). The son of XIVth chief, Ewen Beg McConnell Cameron, and a daughter of MacDougall of Lorne, he was raised by a family of the MacLachlans of Coruanan, hereditary standard bearers to the Camerons of Lochiel. Alongside his former opponent John Dow McEwen Cameron of Erracht, Donald offered fealty to the Earl of Argyll in 1577 (*Argyll Muniments* 148 VII 27; John Stewart of Ardvorlich, 1974 (1981), *The Camerons: A history of Clan Cameron*, 275). This Donald should not be confused with his contemporary Donald Dow McEwen of Erracht.

Moravian - i.e. from Moray in north-east Scotland (Latin, *Moravia*). This supposed origin for the Camerons is dismissed in the standard history of the clan as 'fanciful' (John Stewart of Ardvorlich, *The Camerons*, p5). Early references to the name in Fife and Angus relate to the lordship of the parish of Cameron in Fife. The Cameron chiefly line is usually traced according to the genealogy of 1467MS which has recently been expertly analysed in a pair of articles for *West Highland Notes & Queries* by Ronald Black ('1467 MS: The Camerons (1)', *WHN&Q* Ser.3 No.26, Oct 2014, p3-8; '1467 MS: The Camerons (2)', *WHN&Q* Ser.3 No. 27, April 2015, p3-15). Whatever its ultimate origins, Clan Cameron was a western clan based in Lochaber from at least the fourteenth century.

a kinsman's welcome - Donald McEwen Beg settled in territory controlled by the Earl of Argyll, after offering fealty to him in a Bond of Manrent of 1577 (see note "Donald Dubh" above). Argyll's support for Donald is also noted in *The Memoirs of Sir Ewen Cameron of Lochiel*, p38. It is possible that his connection with the MacLachlans of Coruanan influenced Donald towards Argyll, but he might equally have been motivated by purely political considerations.

the name Ewen is very common - In the traditional Gaelic system of naming, every son of a man named Ewen (Gaelic, *Eoghain*) is known by the patronymic MacEwen (Gaelic, *Mac Eoghain*).

Sir Walter Scott, in the preface to the 1831 edition of *The Fair Maid of Perth*, quotes an opinion that Clan Quhele of Wyntown were the Camerons "who appear to have, about that period, been often designated as MacEwens, and to have gained much more recently the name of Cameron, *i.e.*, crooked nose, from a blemish in the physiognomy of some heroic chief of the line of Lochiel." They were apparently known as MacEwens before they were known as Camerons, but "Camshron" (crooked nose) must have been adopted as their name much earlier, for in 1219 we find the title Ewen de Cambro. From the end of the fourteenth century for a long period the name Ewen is common among the Camerons, both as a first or personal name, and as a surname with the prefix Mac. Since then, there have been four chiefs of the name, of whom one, Sir Ewen Cameron, seventeenth chief, has a distinguished record. Among younger sons, and sons of cadets of the family, there are numerous Ewens. Ewen, the thirteenth chief, by his second wife, Marjory Mackintosh, had a son, also Ewen, the progenitor of the Erracht family, known as "Sliochd Eoghain." Ewen "Beag," fourteenth chief, met an early death. He had a natural son by a daughter of MacDougall of Lorne, Domhnull MacEoghain-Bhig, Donald MacEwen Beg, better known as "Taillear Dubh," and Mac-Dhomh'uill Duibh (Black Donald), a celebrated warrior. So successful was he that he was suspected of a fairy origin, which gave him a special charm, and he has been the subject of much romantic history. He it was, who, getting tired of fighting, retired for a time to a monastery in Cowal, but subsequently returned to the world, married and settled in that district, and left issue.* The Rev.

* Mrs. Mary Mackellar's Traditions.

quotes an opinion - Scott names his source as 'Robert Mackay of Thurso, in his very curious *History of the House and Clan of Mackay*'. Mackay devotes several pages to the question of Clan Quhele, concluding 'There is, in fine, the most cogent reasons to think, that the opponents of the Mackintoshes were the clan Cameron' (p52). Others have suggested that the Battle of North Inch was fought between rival factions within Clan Chattan.

designated as MacEwens - Scott is following Mackay of Thurso (p52), who writes, 'It has been noticed, that the clan Cameron have been designed MacEwan' and speculates that this might be derived not from Ewen but from the forename Hugh or Aodh. There seems no reason to think that Makay is basing his observation on anything beyond the common occurrence of the patronymic McEwen among Camerons, and the existence of the sept *Sliochd Eoghain mhic Eoghain* (for which see note "the Erracht family" below).

known as MacEwens before they were known as Camerons - R. S. T. MacEwen is here following Scott, who in turn is following Mackay. Mackay's original reference in fact suggests that the clan might once have been known as MacAodhan (i.e. *not* MacEwen), which he considers might have given rise to the written form Clan Quhele (see note "designated as MacEwens" above). R. S. T. MacEwen also believed his opinion was supported by Keltie, but see notes "Keltie" above, p18, and "On the conquest of Argyll by Alexander II." above, p5.

the Erracht family - The family of Ewen McEwen Cameron of Erracht is traditionally known in Gaelic as *Sliochd Eoghain mhic Eoghain*, 'the descendants of Ewen son of Ewen'. The same family is referred to in a letter of 1566 as 'clane Ewyn WcEwyn' (NAS GD112/39/12/8; Jane E. A. Dawson (ed.), 1997, *Campbell Letters 1559-1583*, No.81) and in another of 1570 as 'Clan Ewin WikEwin' (NAS GD112/39/7/21; *Campbell Letters*, No.110). John Bodach, the son of John McEwen Cameron of Erracht, appears in two separate documents dated 1598 and 1612 under the name John McVcEwen instead of the expected patronymic John McAne, clearly indicating that the sept name McVcEwen was used within Clan Cameron as a personal appellation (*Privy Council of Scotland*, Vol.V p498-9; *Privy Council of Scotland*, Vol.IX p337). The 'McEwen' name here originates with Ewen McEwen Cameron of Erracht and is not connected with any other MacEwen origins; Ewen McEwen was known by the patronymic 'McEwen' after his father, Ewen McAllan or Allanson, XIIIth chief of Clan Cameron. The eighteenth century armiger William Macewan of Glenboig may have been descended from this sept (see note "Glenboig, County of Stirling" below, p44).

Domhnull Mac-Eoghain-Bhig - Donald McEwen Beg, *an Taillear Dubh*, erroneously referred to above as 'Donald Dubh' (see note "Donald Dubh" above, p19).

Mac-Dhomh'uill Duibh - This is the traditional Gaelic designation of the Cameron chiefs meaning 'the son of Donald Dow (Black Donald)', but the title was never officially held by Donald McEwen Beg.

Mrs. Mary Mackellar - Mary Mackellar wrote a fascinating letter to the editor of *The Celtic Magazine*, relating detailed traditions about Donald McEwen Beg, whose withdrawal from clan politics in 1577 was apparently sudden and gave rise to considerable speculation among his supporters, including the suggestion that he had retired to a monastery (*The Celtic Magazine*, Vol.8, 1883 p268-74.). Mackenzie later drew uncritically on Mackellar's traditions in his *History of the Camerons*.

Malcolm Campbell Taylor, D.D., Professor of Church History, Edinburgh University, is said to be a descendant of his—the name Taylor being derived from "Taillear."

Keltie also has it that after the breaking-up of the Otter clan some followed MacDougall Campbell of Craignish into Lochaber. Could this have been the MacDougall of Lorne—Donald MacEwen Beg—whose daughter was the mother of the "Taillear Dubh?"

In 1576-77 we find one—"Allaster M'Ewin of Camroun,"—applying to the Lords of Council for release from the Earl of Athole, who held him and others in confinement at Blair Athole. Again in 1598 there was a raid by the Lochaber clans on the Dunbars of Moyness, which formed the subject of complaint to the Privy Council, and among those charged are a number of MacEwens.

But these are not the only traditionary and historical instances of connection between the Camerons and the Western Celts. According to the best received Cameron tradition, the first Cameron, already referred to, was a western Celt from Dumbartonshire. An early tradition is that he was a younger son of the Royal Family of Denmark, who came over in 404 to assist Fergus II.; that he married the daughter and heiress of MacMartin of Letterfinlay, and thus acquired the property and chiefship of the clan; and that he was called "Camshron," in Gaelic, from his crooked nose.* The author of the Memoirs of Sir Ewen Cameron and modern clan authorities, however, favour

* As to the way clan pedigrees were constructed in ancient times, see Skene's *Celtic Scotland*, and *Clans Past and Present* in *The Celtic Monthly* for May, 1899, p. 148.

Keltie also has it - Keltie says no such thing. He is discussing the dispersal of the group referred to by Skene as Siol Gillevray (see note "On the conquest of Argyll by Alexander II." above, p5).

MacDougall of Lorne - The MacDougalls of Lorne are chiefs of Clan MacDougall, an entirely separate clan from the MacDougalls of Craignish who are recognised as a cadet branch within Clan Campbell (see notes "Others joined ... " and "MacDougal Campbell of Craignish" above, p7). Therefore, the answer to R. S. T. MacEwen's question is categorically, 'No'. Furthermore, MacDougall of Lorne was not the same person as Donald McEwen Beg (see note "Donald Dubh" p19), as R. S. T. MacEwen appears to suggest, but was in fact his maternal grandfather.

Allaster McEwin - In this document, 'Allaster Dow McAllane McEwin of Camroun, and John Cam, his brother of surnawm' are denounced for the murder of 'Donald Dow McKewin' (J H Burton & D Masson (eds.), 1878-98, *Register of the Privy Council of Scotland*, 1st Series, II, 587-8, 589). Allaster and John are the sons of Allan McAne of Callart, whose father John McAllan was a younger brother of Ewen McAllan, XIIIth chief of Clan Cameron. Their victim Donald Dow McEwen Cameron of Erracht, was assassinated at Inverlochy Castle in 1570. For more detailed analysis of these events, see my *The Erracht Feud* (John Thor Ewing, 2016, *The Erracht Feud: Internal divisions in Clan Cameron 1567-77*).

Again in 1598 - 'Johnne Badach McVcEwene of Errach, [and] his brother Ewne' both took part in the Moyness Raid alongside their chief 'Allane Camroun of Locheldy' (*Privy Council of Scotland*, V, 498-9). These were both sons of John Dow McEwen Cameron of Erracht, younger brother of Donald Dow (d.1570). In 1577, John Dow McEwen had offered fealty to the Earl of Argyll alongside his erstwhile enemy, Donald McEwen Beg (see note "Donald Dubh" above, p19).

According to the best received Cameron tradition - It is unclear what R. S. T. MacEwen's purpose is in recounting these tales of Cameron origins but, for a more recent study of Cameron genealogy, see the recent articles for *West Highland Notes & Queries* by Ronald Black cited in the note "Moravian" above, p19. Much in the next few pages is of uncertain relevance to MacEwen history.

the later tradition, that the first Cameron was a Celt and not a Dane; and the chief has been handed down in history as of Celtic origin. The "crooked nose," as we shall see, had no connection with a Prince of Denmark. The later tradition will be found set out at length in Mackenzie's *History of the Camerons*. Shortly stated, it is this:—"The first Cameron was much renowned for feats in arms and prodigious strength, marvellous instances of which are given. He entered the lists with the most famous champions of his day. In one of these encounters he received a violent blow on the nose, which set it awry, and from this circumstance he was called 'Camshron,' or Cameron, 'Knight of the crooked nose.' The name was, therefore, not Danish, or a first or personal name, but a Gaelic sobriquet arising out of the injury to his nose." The tradition proceeds:—"Our hero was now arrived at the thirty-fifth year of his age, and had given many signal proofs of his valour, so that his name became terrible all over the country. But having little or no paternal estate, he began to think it highly necessary for him to join himself to some great and powerful family, the better to enable him to distinguish himself more eminently than it was possible for him to do as a single man, without friends or relations, or at least such as were of little or no account. He had spent his life in the shire of Dumbarton; but as he had no family or inheritance to encumber him, he resolved to try his fortune in the world and go in search of a wife. He set out accordingly, and happened to light on that part of the country where Lochiel's estate now lies. Here he informed himself of the character and circumstances of the chief who resided there, and understood that he was a man of a large estate, and

Fig.1: Shield of Ewing, 1566.

Fig.2: Shield of John Mackewan of Muckley, 1743.

Fig.3: Shield of William Macewan of Glenboig, 1796.

had a great number of friends and dependents, and withal had a fair and excellent young lady to his daughter. This was a foundation sufficient for our Crooked-Nose Knight to build his hopes and future expectations upon. He made himself known to the chief, and as his fame as a warrior and man of great strength had preceded him, he was well received and hospitably entertained. This chief was MacMartin, Baron of Letterfinlay, and chief of a clan in Lochaber at that time. In short, a bargain was soon struck for the daughter, who was as well pleased as the father with the offer of a husband so much to her liking; for strength of body, vigorous and sinewy limbs, and undaunted courage, were in those days the best qualifications to recommend a man to the affections of a lady. Having married the daughter and led the clan in all their battles against neighbouring tribes and enemies with conspicuous success, he eventually attained to the chiefship." This is the story which the Highland bards have recorded of this great progenitor of the Camerons.

Here we find not a Danish Prince of 404, arriving under kingly protection, and with an introduction from Fergus II., but a Celtic adventurer, many centuries later, from Dumbartonshire. Of his family history nothing is stated, but he was without estate or powerful relatives or friends. He was a soldier of fortune, and he was successful. From the time he assumed the chiefship, the Clan MacMartin and its dependent septs became known as Clan 'Camshron' or Cameron.

This chief was not only skilful in war, but was a man of powerful physique and giant strength. Dumbartonshire in early times appears to have been the

Fig.4: Shield of John McEwan, 1847.

Fig.5: Shield of William McEwan, 1886.

Fig.6: Shield of Robert Finnie McEwen, 1908.

home of Celtic giants. We have this Cambro able to lift a 500lb. stone with the greatest ease. In the New Statistical Account of Scotland (Parish of Luss), we are told it was a place of refuge for the Highlanders from the earliest times. A powerful tribe of Celts lived at Dumfin, where there are traces of an ancient fortification. The chief, Fian M'Cuel, or Fingal, and his associates are represented as giants, of whom the most extravagant feats are related. An enormous stone or mass of rock is pointed out, which, it is said, Fingal, standing on the top of Benbui, took upon his little finger to throw to the top of Shantran Hill, a distance of several miles, but that not being rightly balanced, it fell into a small brook midway between the two! Then there is the tradition of the MacEwen giant who carried a stone coffin from the loch to the churchyard at Luss—having the coffin under one arm and the lid under the other. There is a curious similarity in these various feats of strength. Allowing for the necessary amount of fiction attaching to legends of the kind, we may fairly assume that these early western Celts were a powerful race, so distinguished for athletic performances as to render these worthy of transmission in Celtic folklore. It seems not improbable, too, having regard to the Cameron tradition, that Cambro was of this race of Celtic giants.

It is not stated when Cambro appeared in Lochaber, but it is evident that it could not have been so early as the time of Fergus II. (404), nor even many centuries later, nor yet so late as the close of the 14th century. It is more likely to have been in the twelfth century. Originally the septs of Clan Chattan and Clan Cameron followed the Maormor of Moray; and, according to Gregory, separated about the middle

Fian McCuel, or Fingal - It need hardly be said that we have fully entered the realms of legend at this point. Any connection between the legendary hero Fionn mac Cumhaill and MacEwen history must be extremely tenuous.

the MacEwen giant - This story (see above, p12-3) seems to have had a special significance for R. S. T. MacEwen, and it is possible he learned it from his father. Tales of strong giants are common to the folklore of every nation, but it may be that MacEwen's story of the stone coffin could have been influenced by earlier tales of Fionn mac Cumhaill.

of the fourteenth century. Mackenzie points out that Gregory, who agrees with the other authorities, states that the Camerons, as far back as he could trace, had their seat in Lochaber, and appeared to have been first connected with the Macdonalds of Islay in the reign of Robert the Bruce—that is to say, in the beginning of the fourteenth century.

In 1396, according to MacKenzie, there were four septs or branches of the clan, viz.: Gillanfhaigh or Gillonie (Camerons of Invermalie and Strone), the Clan Soirlie (Camerons of Glen Nevis), MhicMhartain (MacMartins of Letterfinlay), of which Cambro had been chief, and the Camerons of Lochiel. There were also dependent septs, the principal being Mhic Gilveil, or MacMillans. It is said to have been the head or captain of the first of these, Gillanfhaigh (MacGillonies) or Maclanfhaigh—'Fhaigh' in its aspirated form being represented by 'Hay' or 'Kay' of the Chroniclers— who led the Camerons at the Inch of Perth.

Bancho (Shakspeare's Banquo), who was Thane of Lochaber in the time of King Duncan, and was slain by Macbeth because he was foretold that Bancho's posterity would be kings of Scotland—a prophecy which was fulfilled—had a sister Marion who married Angus, the first of the Cameron chiefs of whom there is any mention. From Bancho's grandson Walter, Great Steward of Scotland—an office which became hereditary and was turned into a surname—the Royal Stewart family and the Stewart Earls of Lennox were descended. Then, at a much later period, viz., in 1546, we find 'Ewen Eoghain MacAilein,' the 13th Cameron chief, supporting the then Stewart Earl of Lennox in his rebellion, for which he was tried and executed. Here we have another instance of close

Fig.7: Crest of Ewing of Keppoch and Craigtoun.

Fig.8: Crest of MacEwen.

the then Stewart Earl of Lennox in his rebellion - Matthew Stewart (or Stuart), Earl of Lennox (1516-71) lived as an exile in England, from where he backed King Henry VIII in the War of the Rough Wooing (see note "another instance of close connection between the Lochaber and Dumbartonshire chiefs and clans." below, p25).

connection between the Lochaber and Dumbartonshire chiefs and clans.

All these traditions and historic incidents point to a very early connection between the western clans and those known at a later period as Camerons. If Keltie and the historian quoted by Sir Walter Scott be correct, the MacEwens in their early wanderings had first settled in Lochaber, and were the progenitors of the later Camerons. This would account for the name among the Camerons as early as the 13th century. Cambro was of the same race, and may have been of the same tribe. The name Ewen, while it has been common in the Cameron families and in Lochaber, is rare among the neighbouring clans of the district who were connected with the Camerons under Moravian rule. It is not a common name among the Mackintoshes, or the other septs of Clan Chattan or the Moravian clans. It is of western origin, and common among the western clans. In later times, the families of that name in Lochaber appear to have derived it, in some cases, from the Cameron Ewens, according to Celtic custom, for the "Sliochd Eoghain" were the children and descendants of the first Ewen, chief of Erracht. In others, it doubtless had its origin in the later connection with the Macdougall Campbells of Lorne; and the "Sliochd Eoghain" was probably composed of the descendants of both.

The Privy Council Records afford further evidence of this close intermixture of MacEwens and Camerons. In 1576 we find Allister Dow Mc Allane Vc Ewin Camroun and John Camroun, his brother, denounced for the slaughter of Donald Dow McKewin. In 1598, there was a complaint before the Council at the instance of George Dunbar in Clunes and others

another instance of close connection between the Lochaber and Dumbartonshire chiefs and clans. - There is no 'close connection' of the kind that R. S. T. MacEwen asserts between Lochaber and Dumbartonshire, and the notion that Ewen McAllan XIII opposed the King of Scots in 1546 because of a remote connection with the earldom of Lennox is not credible. As early as 1503, Ewen McAllan Cameron had supported Donald Dow MacDonald in his bid for the Lordship of the Isles. In the 1540's, he supported Donald's successor James MacDonald of Dunniveg because he was, as he wrote in a letter to the Lord Deputy of Ireland, 'narrest of Ayr to the hous of the Ylies' (Stewart of Ardvorlich, *The Camerons*, p27); the involvement of the Earl of Lennox in this struggle was merely incidental.

between the western clans and those known at a later period as Camerons - R. S. T. MacEwen seems to have settled on a particular 'prehistory' for Clan Cameron which separates them from other 'western' clans but, at least as far as their known history in Lochaber is concerned, Clan Cameron would usually be considered a western clan, so their association with other western clans is unremarkable.

If Keltie and the historian quoted by Sir Walter Scott be correct - Neither of these historians makes the case which R. S. T. MacEwen suggests. Keltie (following Browne and Skene) describes the dispersion of the group identified by Skene as Siol Gillevray into the various clans of recorded history (see note "On the conquest of Argyll by Alexander II." above, p5). To number Clan Ewen of Otter amongst the clans descended from Siol Gillevray, would require the rejection of the only surviving genealogy of the clan, but even this would not suggest that the clan had any direct connection with Lochaber, and it would certainly not link MacEwens from Lochaber with descendants of Clan Ewen of Otter. Likewise Mackay, 'the historian quoted by Sir Walter Scott', does not suggest that the clan name Cameron masks a deeper MacEwen identity, and certainly not an identity that might be linked with MacEwens from Cowal, Argyll or other parts of Scotland.

This would account for the name - The McEwen name exists as a patronymic in Clan Cameron for the simple reason that the name Ewen is relatively common as a forename in the clan. Any man whose father was called Ewen Cameron was known by the patronymic McEwen, just as any man whose father was called Allan Cameron was known by the patronymic McAllan, but in neither case would this in any way affect their clan identity as a Cameron.

neighbouring clans of the district ... under Moravian rule - These are the clans of the Chattan Federation, in particular Clan MacIntosh, traditional enemies of Clan Cameron. One would not necessarily expect traditional enemies to share naming traditions. See note "Moravian" above, p19.

the first Ewen, chief of Erracht - Ewen McEwen Cameron of Erracht, son of Ewen McAllan of Lochiel, XIIIth chief of Clan Cameron, thought by Gregory to have been assassinated at Inverlochy in 1570, but actually died before 1567 (Donald Gregory, 1836 (1881), *History of the Western Highlands & Isles of Scotland, 1493-1625*, p229; John Thor Ewing, 2016, *The Erracht Feud*).

the Macdougall Campbells of Lorne - The term 'MacDougalls of Lorne' would usually indicate an entirely separate clan from the MacDougalls or Campbells of Craignish, who appear to be meant here. Neither clan can be descended from Clan Ewen of Otter as R. S. T. MacEwen suggests (see notes "Others joined ..." and "MacDougal Campbell of Craignish" above, p7).

"Sliochd Eoghain" - The Gaelic term *Sliochd Eoghain mhic Eoghain* (rendered in sixteenth-century Scots as 'Clan Ewen Vic Ewen', see note "the Erracht family" above, p20), specifically refers to the descendants of Ewen McEwen Cameron of Erracht and their followers, and does not include members of other unrelated clans.

close intermixture of MacEwens and Camerons - R. S. T. MacEwen seems confused by the occurrence of the patronymic McEwen within clan Cameron. There is no 'intermixture' of clans, but Cameron clansmen (who drew on a limited stock of forenames) are regularly distinguished from one another by their patronymics. See note "This would account for the name" above.

Allister Dow McAllane - see note "Allaster McEwin" above, p21.

In 1598 - see note "Again in 1598" above, p21.

against Ewne McConeill Vc Ewne Coneill of Blarmaseylach, John Badach Mc Vc Ewne of Errach, his brother Ewne, Duncane Mc Martin of Letterfinlay, and many other MacEwens, who are described as "200 brokin hieland men and sorneris, all bodin in feir of weir." The charge against them gives a picturesque view of the occupations of our ancestors. Armed " with bows, darlochs, and twa-handit swords, steil bonnetis, haberschondes, hacquebutis and pistoletis," they are accused of having " come under cloud and silence of night be way of briggandice" to the house of the said George Dunbar, where they committed sundry offences of which the discreet historian need make no mention. Some years later we find these MacEwens allied with the outlawed MacGregors. In 1612 there is an order to denounce John Camroun Mc Vc Ewne in Errach and others for refusing to concur with Lochiel against " the rebellious thieves and lymmaris of the Clan Gregour." Again, in the same year, several MacEwens are fined for resetting and defending Clan Gregor. In the following year there is a solemn proclamation against Allan Cameron of Locheil for not taking measures against the MacGregors, the preamble declaring that " he has made shipwraik of his faith and promisit obedience, shaking off all feir of God and his prince and reverence of the law; and preferring the mischevious and unhappy course of his bypast wicked lyff to godliness, civilite, good reule and quietness." As associates in this " mischevious and unhappy course of bypast wickedness " are enumerated several MacEwens, whose affection for the 'lymmaris' of Clan Gregor would seem to have been incorrigible.

In consequence of an old feud between the

many other MacEwens - It should go without saying that, like the MacMartins of Letterfinlay, these men owed allegiance to Clan Cameron. Whereas the MacMartins are an allied clan with a separate agnatic line, the MacEwens of *Sliochd Eoghain* in Clan Cameron are a cadet branch descended via Ewen McEwen of Erracht from the XIIIth Cameron chief, Ewen McAllan of Lochiel (see notes "the Erracht family" above, p20, "Sliochd Eoghain" above, p26).

200 brokin ... weir - 'Two hundred outlaw Highland men and robbers, all provided with warlike array' (*Privy Council of Scotland*, Vol.V p498-9). Although 'broken' can also mean 'lordless', on this occasion the men are riding out with their chief, Allan McConnell Dow Cameron XVI.

with bows ... pistoletis - 'with bows, quivers (arrow holsters), and two-handed swords, steel bonnets (helmets), habergeons (mail shirts), harquebusses (an early form of musket) and pistols"

briggandice - 'brigandry, robbery'

1612 - At this time, the Earl of Huntly was deliberately sowing dissension between the various branches of Clan Cameron.

John Camroun Mc Vc Ewne in Errach - This is John Bodach and, in this case, 'McVcEwen' is not a patronymic (see note "the Erracht family" above, p20). The other potential 'MacEwens' named include John's brother, Ewne Camroun, and Johnne McDonnald Camroun, who is described as his brother's son but might in fact be the son of his uncle Donald Dow, the confusion arising from the fact that John's father was also John McVcEwen; there is also a Ewne McDonnald VcEwne Camroun in Blairniscalloch (*Register of the Privy Council*, Vol.IX p337).

a solemn proclamation - *Register of the Privy Council*, Vol.X p185-9

several MacEwens - At this point in Cameron history, the McEwens of *Sliochd Eoghain* may indeed have regarded themselves as a distinct sept within Clan Cameron, but they are nonetheless Camerons by ancestry and are not related to Clan Ewen of Otter (see notes "the Erracht family" above, p20, "Sliochd Eoghain" above, p26).

Camerons and the Robertsons of Struan, Sir Ewen Cameron, in 1666, marched with 80 men to Struan's lands in Kinloch, and raided the Robertsons. Among them were two MacEwen Camerons, John and Duncan, dhuine vassals. This formed the subject of a trial before the Privy Council.

VII.—MacEwens in Perthshire, Inverness, and Skye.

From an early date, a branch of the MacEwens appears to have been settled in Perthshire, probably in the Kenmore district, and a curious legend is connected with their early history. The original head of the clan in Perthshire died, leaving two sons. He left also a beautiful white horse, the possession of which occasioned a dispute between the two sons. The matter was decided by a singular test, namely, who could roll a millstone down a certain mountain by means of a straw rope passed through the hole in the centre. The one son accomplished the feat and obtained the horse. The other, being unsuccessful, betook himself to Ayrshire, where he founded another branch of the family.* However unsound the story may be as a genealogical explanation, it points to a traditional relationship existing between remote branches of the family at a time when their early origin was lost in tradition.

From Perthshire or Lochaber the MacEwens spread northwards. At an early date the name appears among the Mackintosh genealogies. "About this time (circa 1370) also lived Kenneth Macewn,

*This legend has been kindly furnished by Dr. David MacEwan, who obtained it in 1847 from an octogenarian soldier of the name of MacEwan.

dhuine vassals - 'gentlemen' (see note "dhuin vassals" above, p16). They are presumably sons of the XVIIth chief Sir Ewen Cameron of Lochiel and, as such, go by the patronymic 'McEwen'.

a branch of the MacEwens - This reflects R. S. T. MacEwen's belief in a MacEwen exodus from Argyll.

Perthshire - There is still an extensive McEwan population in Perthshire, descended from 'The Mac Ewens of Achomer, Perth, and Dungarthill' who appear in the *List of the different Clans and Tribes descended from the Family of Lorne*. In the early nineteenth century, they appear to have used the names MacEwen and MacDougall interchangeably, and were said to 'still occupy Achomer, Claggan, and Milton Ardtalnaig' (Robert Craig Maclagan, 1905, *The Perth Incident of 1396*, p341-5 cf. p306). The existence of a MacEwen cadet branch within Clan MacDougall is fully supported by MacDougall tradition, which acknowledges MacEwans in Argyll as descended from this clan. Its chieftain, who traced his descent from the chiefs of Clan MacDougall, lived at Dungarthill and registered arms as Mackewan of Muckley in 1743 (see notes "nine grants of arms" below, p34 and "The Muckly family" below, p35). I am grateful to Thomas Ashby McCown for information from a Cowan family in Virginia, whose traditions say that 'they lived, ... in Kilchrenan [in Lorne, Argyll], below Mt Cruachan, [and] ... are descended from King Ewan and connected in some way to the senior MacDougall cadet branch.' A confusion may have arisen between Ewen Mor MacDougall, King of the Isles, and Ewen Mor MacDougall of Ballinreoch (see note "Muckly, County of Argyll" below, p44), but the tradition of descent from King Ewen Mor MacDougall may have been widespread in Lorne, and potentially indicates a much earlier origin for the MacEwen name.

a curious legend - Ayrshire McEwens could equally have come from Galloway (see note "Girvan, Ayrshire" above, p14). The first reference to McEwens in Ayrshire concerns George Makewin, a follower of the Earl of Cassilis, respited for murder in 1526 (*Register of the Privy Seal*, Vol.I No.3386). In 1622, John Kennedy, Earl of Cassilis, is served heir to a McEwinstoun in Ayrshire (*Inquisitionum ad Capellam Domini Regis retornatarum*, Vol.I 'Ayr' No.212). The McEwens of Bardrochat trace their ancestry to a James McEwen (b.1695) drowned in the River Stinchar in 1737 (or possibly 1731). Current Bardrochat tradition is that three McEwen brothers came by boat from the Highlands—if so, this must have been before 1737 but probably after 1695, since James's father John is not recorded in the family bible as 'in Bardrochat'. Their arrival by boat is plausible but this tradition may been influenced by clan history books, so whether they came from the Highlands to the north or from the nearby Rhins of Galloway to the south remains an open question.

spread northwards - This too reflects R. S. T. MacEwen's unfounded assumption that all MacEwens originate in a single clan in Cowal, Argyll, rather than arising independently in the north.

Mackintosh genealogies - The genealogy quoted here is of course for Clan Macpherson. This early MacEwen connection is noted by Alexander Nisbet (*A System of Heraldry*, 1722, p415), who writes of the three sons of Ewan Ban Macpherson saying, 'From Kenneth, the eldest, is come the family of Clunie, which was then and since known by the name of McEwen.' Nisbet's assertion is confirmed by the Invereshie Book Genealogy (c.1704), where two important kindreds are noted among the oldest of the clan, being Clan Vc Ewen Dow (Gaelic, *Clann Mhic Eoghain Duibh* or in the spelling of the text, 'Clan vic Ewan duy') and Clan Vc Ewen Tailor (Gaelic, *Clann Mhic Eoghain Taillear*, or 'Clan vic Ewan taylor'); other references to McEwins in this text are thought to refer to members of this clan. The Ardross Manuscript (1687) likewise confirms the genealogy of Clan Ewen Tailor and Clan Ewen Dow ('the clan Ewin Taileur & the clan Ewin due'). The Kinrara Manuscript (c.1680) sees the clan (traditionally split into the three families of Cluny, Pitmain and Invereshie) as divided into three MacEwen groups: 'Slighk Kynich vic Ewin'; 'Slighk ean vic Ewin'; and 'Slighk Gillies vic Ewin'. These 'MacEwen' clans are of course better known as Clan Macpherson and have no connection with either Clan Cameron or Clan Ewen of Otter.

Another unrelated Lochaber MacEwen connection is seen in the Macleans of Ardgour who go by the Gaelic name *Mac 'ic Eoghain* (J. G. Campbell, 1895, *Clan traditions and popular tales of the western Highlands and islands*, p4) and likewise Maclean's Tower on Loch Linnhe is known in Gaelic as *Tubhailt Mhic'ic Eoghain*. Ewen Maclean II of Ardgour from whom they take their name was Seneschal to the Lord of the Isles, and appears in records between 1463 and 1495.

father of Parson. This Kenneth came from Lochaber in Badenoch, and dwelt first at Tullocher. He was a tenant and retainer of Lauchlan, laird of Mackintosh. But his brothers, John, Murrach, and Gillies, came thither long before that time. This Lauchlan, 8th laird of Mackintosh, passed away from among the living in the year of Christ 1407."* A daughter of Ferquhard, 9th laird of Mackintosh, married Duncan Mackynich vic Ewen (commonly called Parson). To Malcolm, 10th laird of Mackintosh (died 1470), Charles MacEwen vic Volan subscribed for himself and his posterity as hereditary servant. In 1569 the laird of Mackintosh leased to Donald MacEwen *alias* Cameron and John, his brother, the lands of Glenlui and Locharkaig. In 1618 there was a complaint to the Privy Council by Lord Gordon against Sir Lauchlan Mackintosh in the matter of "a riot and tumult at the ford of Culloden" to prevent Lord Gordon exercising his right to collect the teinds of the parish of Inverness. MacEwens were conspicuous among the followers of Mackintosh, who, to quote the report, "in a grite rage, tumult, and furie, attacked Lord Gordon's poore hairmless men."

A considerable body of MacEwens appear to have been settled in Skye at one time. It is not stated when their first settlement there took place; but from General Wade's Statement of the Highland Clans in 1715, there were 150 MacEwens then in the Island, who fought for King James in that year. The colony may have been derived either from the Otter or Lochaber families, or both. There is a tradition, unsupported however by documentary evidence, that 120 of the Skye MacEwens fought for Prince Charlie

* *Macfarlane's Genealogical Collections* (Scot. Hist Soc.)

A daughter ... hereditary servant - Two more of the many people who have had a father or grandfather called Ewen (Gaelic, *Eoghain*) and who, in consequence, are named in Gaelic as *Mac Eoghain* or *Mhic Eoghain*. See note "This would account for the name" above, p26.

Donald MacEwen alias Cameron and John, his brother - These are the sons of Ewen McEwen Cameron of Erracht, see note "the Erracht family" p20, above; see also Ewing, 2016, *The Erracht Feud*.

MacEwens were conspicuous - The only 'MacEwen' involved would appear to have been 'Ewine McEwne McMurriche' who is mentioned three times in connection with the incident (*Register of the Privy Council*, Vol.XI, p479-80). Ewine's name is given in the form of a patronymic, indicating that his father was called Ewne McMurriche; both men might also have used the clan name MacIntosh.

Skye - This reference to Wade is found in James Logan's book *The Scottish Gaël* (Edinburgh, 1831) but is not traceable beyond this. Logan presumably misread Wade's reference to 150 'McLeans in the Isle of Skye' in his *Report on the Highlands* of 1724. There is no evidence for a MacEwen community on Skye.

120 of the Skye MacEwens - This must be a misremembered version of Logan's original mistake; there were no more MacEwens on Skye in 1745 than there had been in 1715.

at Culloden. If this be true it is curious that there is no record of an event so comparatively recent. In the *List of Persons Concerned in the Rebellion of 1745* (Scot. Hist. Soc.), the strength of the clan in rebellion is given at 5, and of the four MacEwens mentioned by name, two hail from Stirling, one from Perth, and one from Dundee. The *List* is obviously incomplete, as the total number of the clans is only given as 780.*

VIII.—The Clan Name.

The name Ewen is a distinctive, ancient, and not very common name, derived from the Gaelic *Eoghan*, meaning 'kind natured' (latin *Eugenius*). Clan names were derived from the personal or first name of the ancestral chief, with the prefix 'Mac.' In later times, for special or fanciful reasons, the 'Mac' was often dropped, and the personal name became the surname. This was more particularly the case when persons of Highland descent, bearing clan names, settled in the Lowlands. The name MacGregor is a good instance of this change. When the clan name became proscribed, the clansmen called themselves Gregors, Gregs, Doos, and other forms of the name. Mr. Adam says: "two reasons have contributed towards rendering obscure the origin of Highland names of clan origin; the villainous and erratic spelling of our ancestors, and the clothing of a Highland name in a Lowland garb, either by dropping the prefix Mac or by otherwise transmogrifying the original name.† A distinguished Gaelic scholar and

* In a note to *Redgauntlet*, Scott says that he believes that the adventure ascribed to Pate-in-Peril, in 1745, was actually undertaken by a gentleman of the name of MacEwen or Macmillan.

† *What is my Tartan?* Frank Adam, F.S.A., Scot.

List of Persons Concerned in the Rebellion of 1745 - The MacEwens listed in this source are:

Perth District: Donald McEwan, mason, Dunkeld, 'Carried Arms in the Rebel Army', current location 'Lurking'

Perth District: John McEwan, residenter in Dunkeld, 'Carried Arms in Rebel Army', current location 'Lurking'

Stirling District: James McEwan, son to John McEwen, shoemaker, Stirling, 'Accepted of a Commission in the Rebel Army', [current location:] 'not known'

Elgine District: John McEvan, Balacherach, 'Carried Arms in said army, was forced out, has submitted to Royal Mercy', [current location:] 'at home'

Dundee District: John McEwan, son to the Laird of Dungarthle [i.e. Dungarthill], Dungarthle, Capoth [i.e. Caputh], Perth, 'was a Lieut. in the rebel army, joined them before Falkirk Battle', [current location:] 'not known'

This may be compared with information from The Jacobite Muster Roll (Aikman, Christian et al. 2001, *No Quarter Given: The Muster Roll of Prince Charles Edward Stuart's Army, 1745-46*, Glasgow (Neil Wilson)):

John McEvan, Bellindrom: Regiment, MacDonell of Glengarry; Surrendered 5 May 1746. Probably released.

Alexander Roy McEvan, W. Dundreggan: Regiment, MacDonell of Glengarry; Surrendered 5 May 1746. Probably released.

William McEvan, Invermoriston: Regiment, MacDonell of Glengarry; Surrendered 5. May 1746. Probably released.

John McEwan ygr of Muchlie: Regiment, John Roy Stuart's (Edinburgh); Killed at Culloden

Kenneth ban MacEwan: Regiment, Robstan McKinnon's: Fate unknown

The Jacobite McEwans from Perth and Stirling probably belonged to the MacEwen sept of Clan MacDougall. 'John McEwan y[oun]g[e]r of Muchlie' who is recorded as 'Killed at Culloden', is the son of the chieftain John Mackewan of Muckley, the first MacEwen armiger (see note "Muckly, County of Argyll" below, p44) and appears in the List of Persons Concerned in the Rebellion as 'John McEwan, son to the Laird of Dungarthle'. According to his descendant Andrew McEwen of Ballinreoch, the widow of John McEwan of Muckley adopted the name of Bell and went into hiding with her young son.

John McEvan in Bellindrom was described in 1746 as 'Pressed. At no Engagement, and of a Suspected Carracter.' Alexander McEvan Roy in 'Vester Dundregon' was said to be 'A Volunteare. Honest.' William McEvan 'Returned after Gladsmuir and never Rose any more in Arms. Honest.' (William Mackay, 1914, *Urquhart and Glenmoriston: Olden times in a Highland parish*, p495-8)

These records are incomplete, so that both lists omit Robert and Gideon McEwen mentioned by Mr. John McEwen above, p16, and others might well be similarly omitted.

Eoghan - There is disagreement as to the origin of the forename Ewen, *Eoghain*. Whilst it might be from Latin *Eugenius*, it is more often thought to derive from Gaelic meaning 'born of the yew' (Black, 1946, *Surnames of Scotland*, p245-6.; Ó Corráin & Maguire, 1981, 1990, *Irish Names*, p87-8).

the 'Mac' was often dropped - Whilst individual members of a clan were known in Gaelic by the clan name with the prefix Mac meaning 'son of' (thus, *Mac Griogair, Mac Dòmhnall, Mac Eoghain*), the clan name itself was commonly given without it (thus, *Clann Griogair, Clann Dòmhnall, Clann Eoghain*). Deriving a Scots surname from a Gaelic clan name thus offered two choices and, where the choice was not to use 'Mac' as seems to have been common at an early period, this does not mean that the clan name has in any way been altered. It may be significant that the Ewing form of the name which distinguishes this clan from other MacEwens, was adopted at the point when the distinctive territorial designation 'of Otter' was no longer available. For the use of the territorial designation 'of Otter' to distinguish the clan from other MacEwens, see 'Introduction', vii.

writer on the subject points out that surnames 'largely depend on individual and local history, being subject to local caprices and 'pet' changes.' In a work on the subject he gives the derivation of this name as above stated.* It would, however, be ridiculous to hold, at the present day, that all persons bearing a clan name are necessarily descendants of the old clansmen. In the majority of cases they probably are: in others the name may have been derived from a different source or taken by an ancestor for a 'special' or 'fanciful' reason. In later times surnames have often been derived from the Christian name of the parent, as MacWilliam and Williamson. Some MacEwen surnames may have had this origin, or in some instances may have been derived from Ian, Ivan, or Ewan in the same way. But in the absence of family histories showing the origin and course of a name, in each case, it is possible to treat the subject only generally, having regard to the localities where the name is common, and to any traditions or information which connect it with these localities. Where the name is of clan origin and still common in the clan territory, and where septs and families can be traced by tradition or otherwise from the original home to other localities where the name is found, while the other names common to those localities are different,—in both these cases there is a *prima facie* presumption that the name has been handed down from the original source, and that those who bear it are the descendants and representatives,—remotely, no doubt,—of the immigrant clansmen. Clan Ewen was a small clan which was dispersed at a remote period, and therefore the only means of identifying present day holders of

* *Personal Names and Surnames in Inverness*: A. Macbain.

in the absence of family histories - In the twenty-first century, we can expect that, alongside traditional genealogy, Y-DNA will play an increasing role in correctly identifying agnatic origins. There is no single haplotype for any clan but, as more data becomes available, the complex picture of how individual lines relate to the clans will inevitably become clearer. Whilst the testimony of DNA may be absolute in determining purely biological ancestry, patterns of kinship and clanship are at least as much a function of society as of biology.

Where the name is of clan origin - It is of course not always possible to tell whether the name is of clan origin. Whereas R. S. T. MacEwen based his work on the assumption that there was a single clan origin for the name, it has now been possible to demonstrate that there were several different origins, reflecting roots in several different clans—none of these alternative origins is compatible with a supposed origin in Clan Ewen of Otter. It may be difficult to assess the relative number of MacEwens who might be descended from each separate origin but, in general, it is sensible to consider origins attested by historical evidence before turning to an origin which is at odds with the evidence:

    For origins in Clan Bisset, see notes "the Black Douglas" p15, "McKeown" p17, "Reviresco" p18;

    For Clan MacDougall, see "Perthshire" p28, "List of Persons Concerned in the Rebellion of 1745" p30, "the Muckly family" p35, "Muckly, County of Argyll" p44;

    For Clan Cameron, see "William MacEwan of Glenboig" p14, "the Erracht family" p20, "Sliochd Eoghain" p26, "Macewan of Glenboig" p35, "Glenboig, County of Stirling" p44;

    For possible origins in Clans Chattan and Maclean, see "Mackintosh genealogies" p28;

    For Ewings as the descendants of Clan Ewen of Otter, see "Sufnee or Swene, the IX. and last of the Otter chiefs" p6, "under a chieftain of their own", "in the fifteenth century", "under Lennox", "where they received a banner" p12, "there is no memorial" p13, "all the arms of the later Ewings" p35, "a hard and checkered existence" p41;

    For another possible origin for the Lowland names Ewen, Ewan and Ewans, see additional notes on p44.

immigrant clansmen - R. S. T. MacEwen imagines an original small core of MacEwens dispersing and expanding over the whole of Scotland.

the name is by tracing the old clansmen to the districts and localities where the name survives.

Lord President Forbes described a 'Highland clan' as a 'set of men all bearing the same surname, and believing themselves to be related the one to the other, and to be descended from the same stock.' Originally Clan Ewen answered this definition—one which is still true, subject to the above considerations. According to Lower, surnames and the practice of transmitting them to descendants came gradually into common use in England as early as the 11th and three following centuries. Other, equally good, authorities hold that not till the time of the Reformation did surnames become established on something like their present footing in England and the lowland counties of Scotland, and at a later period in the Highlands, and there have always been the difficulties connected with spelling, to the confusion of antiquaries and genealogists. This name alone furnishes several variations, viz.: Ewan, Ewen, Ewing, MacEwan, MacEwen, McEwan, McEwen, Macewin, MacKewan, McKewan, McKeown, McEwing, McAine, etc. The original clan name, of course, is Ewen, and Skene and the other authorities so spell it, and the later forms of the name, and those most common at the present day, are Ewen and Ewing, MacEwan and MacEwen, and the abridged form of the two latter: K is the common Irish form. The same variations in spelling have occurred in places widely apart, as Argyll, the Lennox, Galloway, and Lochaber, all of which are associated with the clan. Sometimes *i* is used in place of *a* or *e*, in the last syllable; and where *k* has been used in early, it has been dropped in later, times. Uniformity was the last thing thought of: in the case of father and son,

all bearing the same surname - There are in fact numerous instances where more than one surname is common within a clan. The essential element is kinship, whether real or fictive. R. S. T. MacEwen did a great deal to persuade MacEwens that they were indeed related to one another, but their deeper roots actually link them to families and alliances with entirely different clans.

McAine - The names McAne and McIain are usually derived from Gaelic *Mac Eoin* rather than *Mac Eoghain*, but confusion between these names has always been common.

The original clan name - The name is originally Gaelic and predates any completely regularised spelling system, so no single spelling in either English or Gaelic can be claimed as 'original'.

or in the same family, it was not considered necessary. As a rule, spelling was phonetic, and to this fact may be ascribed the frequent introduction of the K; rather than to any recent Irish connection. Excellent examples are furnished in the Galloway and Glenboig families. In the former the name appears in the family Bibles and on the tombstones in the various forms stated : in the latter we have first Macewin, then in 1691 McAine, and the same man in 1698 as Macewan, while the family history shows continuous descent and succession.*

X.—EVIDENCE OF HERALDRY.

Heraldry is usually a safe and reliable guide in cases of pedigree and enquiries into family histories.

* Uniformity in spelling was not practised by even the best English writers, *e.g.*, Dryden and Driden, Jonson and Johnson. An ingenious American has discovered 4,000 variations of the name Shakespeare.

McAine - This surname usually denotes Gaelic *Mac Eoin* rather than *Mac Eoghain*, but the two names have frequently been confused—see for example above, p13, and note "Baor" above, p15.

a safe and reliable guide - This statement is undoubtedly correct, especially in Scotland where each clan can be easily distinguished by its distinctive heraldry. If R. S. T. MacEwen had begun with heraldry, he would surely have observed that it indicates more than one distinct clan origin for the MacEwen name (see note "all the arms of the later Ewings" below, p35).

There are nine grants of Arms by the Lyon Office in Scotland to persons bearing the clan name. Six of these are Ewings and three McEwans.

One of the earliest is Ewen or Ewing of Craigtoun, whose achievement appears on a tombstone of 1600 in Bonhill Churchyard. These arms belonged originally to Bryson of Craigtoun. In Nisbet's *System of Heraldry* (1722), one of the best authorities on ancient Scottish Heraldry, it is said that these arms are carried by John *Ewen*, Writer to the Signet; and further on, with reference to Bryson of Craigtoun, that "this family ended in two daughters: the eldest married Walter Ewing, Writer to the Signet: they were the father and mother of John Ewing, Writer to the Signet, who possesses the lands of Craigtoun which belonged to his grandfather by the mother's side, and by the father's side he is the male Representer of Ewing of Keppoch, his grandfather, in the Shire of Dumbarton; which lands of Keppoch were purchased by a younger son of the Family, who had only one daughter, married to John Whitehill, whose son Thomas possesses the lands of Keppoch, and is obliged to take upon him the name of Ewing."

These arms then came into the Ewen or Ewing family with the lands of Craigtoun by the marriage of Walter Ewen or Ewing, Writer to the Signet, with the eldest daughter of Bryson. The arms, themselves, throw no light on the family history of the Ewens or Ewings: but the father of Walter Ewen or Ewing was of the Keppoch family in Dumbartonshire. We therefore find this much: (1) that the name was then spelt both ways, and that Ewing or Ewen were interchangeable: and (2) that the family belonged to Dumbartonshire where the clan name was common.

nine grants of arms - R. S. T. MacEwen is considering the period since 1672, when *Lyon Register* begins. He appears to have missed a grant of arms in 1886 to William McEwan and another in 1893 to Charles Lindsay Orr Ewing. It would also seem appropriate now to also include Robert Finnie McEwen of Bardrochat who registered arms with Lyon Court in 1908 (shortly after the original publication of this booklet). For further details see below, p43-4 and accompanying notes.

Bonhill Churchyard - This tombstone (which is now covered either by the enlarged church or by grass) is said by R. S. T. MacEwen to have borne the date 1600, which is before the Ewing family inherited Craigtoun, but see note "Bonhill Churchyard" below, p43.

belonged originally to Bryson of Craigtoun - It is difficult to see how this error has occurred. The Ewing arms are not remotely similar to the arms of Bryson, and it would never be possible to inherit arms without also adopting the associated name (as in the case of John Ewing of Keppoch *alias* Whitehill, 1671-c.1746). The Ewing arms first appear under the name 'Ewing' in the Workman Armorial and may be dated to 1566 (see note "Keppoch" below, p43). If R. S. T. MacEwen had understood the antiquity of the Ewing arms relative to all the arms he lists for the name MacEwen, he might also have realised that, in combination with other evidence, it points to this clan as heirs to Clan Ewen of Otter.

lands of Keppoch - Keppoch House, Cardross, Dumbartonshire (now Argyll & Bute).

Again, all the arms of the later Ewings of Keppoch, Glasgow, Levenfield, Loudon, and Ballikinrain, which are recorded, are founded on and connected with those of the first Ewen or Ewing of Craigtoun.

The three McEwen families return similar results. The Muckly family, in addition to its name and place of settlement in Argyll, claims descent from the MacDougalls of Lorne, who were joined by a sept of Clan MacEwen of Otter. Macewan of Glenboig belonged to the Lennox sept. McEwan, Glasgow, belonged to a Renfrewshire family of the same sept, descended, on the female side again, from a daughter of Campbell of Craignish in Lorne. So that so far as name, localities, and other circumstances go they all point,—in the absence of other evidence,—to one and the same conclusion, viz., that these families are descended from different septs of the ancient Clan Ewen.

There is another circumstance of some importance in this connection, which, although not having modern heraldic sanction, is of the same character. In early times, when writing was not an ordinary or common accomplishment, documents of moment were attested by seals. This practice was common up to 1540 and, as Nisbet says, 'contributed much to the regularity of arms.' It continued down to a much later date, and for some purposes is still in force. These seals bore a device, an animal, tree, shrub, flower, leaf, or other symbol, and sometimes a motto. The devices, again, in later times, became common to connected families and persons of the same name who recognised a clan relationship, until at last they have come to be spoken of and used as 'clan crests.' But their original purpose was altogether different. Seals were handed down from

all the arms of the later Ewings - From the evidence cited by R. S. T. MacEwen on the previous page, it will be seen that the family of Ewing of Keppoch was in fact ancestral to the Ewings of Craigtoun. All these coats of arms are based on the arms of Ewing recorded in the Workman Armorial in 1566 (see note "Keppoch" below, p43). As is to be expected in Scottish heraldry, all the heraldic achievements within a clan make use of the same heraldic devices and are easily recognised as a coherent group. The Ewing arms constitute an independent heraldic tradition representing an independent clan. Arms recorded for the name MacEwen do not all form a coherent group, and so do not represent arms awarded within a single clan.

The three McEwen families - Heraldry for the MacEwen name begins with the grant of arms in 1743 to John Mackewan of Muckley. His arms identified him within the traditions of Clan MacDougall—he bears the MacDougall lion in chief, with a distinctive garb or wheat sheaf in base. By contrast, the next MacEwen armiger, William Macewan of Glenboig, 1796, adopts arms indicating his allegiance as a Cameron. In 1847 however, when the industrialist John McEwan was granted arms, the lion and garb from the arms of Mackewan of Muckley were understood to represent the name McEwan, and so a distinctive heraldic tradition was apparently established.

The Muckly family - Mackewan of Muckley (see note "Muckly, County of Argyll" below, p44). Muckley is in Perthshire, not Argyll; Mill of Muckly is adjacent to the family seat of Dungarthill. James McEwan of Muckly is listed as Commissary Clerk of Dunkeld, Perthshire, in 1759. John Mackewan of Muckley's achievement of arms reflects his status as chieftain of a sept of Clan MacDougall, and his descent from the MacDougall chiefs (see note "Perthshire" above, p28).

joined by a sept - There is no evidence that there were ever any septs of Clan Ewen of Otter. The suggestion that Clan MacDougall was 'joined' by such a sept is entirely unfounded. Mackewan of Muckley took his name from his ancestor Ewen Mor MacDougall of Ballinreoch and not because of an imagined link with a supposed sept of an unrelated clan. R. S. T. MacEwen's mistake arises from his misreading of Keltie, who discusses the possibility that an entirely different clan, the MacDougalls of Craignish, not Lorne (see notes "Others joined..." and "MacDougal Campbell of Craignish" above, p7) might be descended from Siol Gillevray, not from Clan Ewen of Otter (see note "On the conquest of Argyll by Alexander II." above, p5).

Macewan of Glenboig - William Macewan of Glenboig did not belong to any sept of the clan imagined by R. S. T. MacEwen, and his achievement of arms unambiguously declares his allegiance to Clan Cameron. He is presumably descended from *Sliochd Eoghain* (see notes "the Erracht family" above, p20, "Sliochd Eoghain" above, p26). The Glenboig from which he derived his territorial designation is in Lanarkshire (see note "William MacEwan of Glenboig" above, p14).

descended, on the female side - John McEwan's great grandfather, also called John McEwan, married Anna Campbell, daughter of Campbell of Craignish in 1724. This connection has no bearing on his McEwan heritage, and his Campbell inheritance is referenced separately in his heraldic Bordure (see note "Glasgow" below, p44). Surnames are not inherited through the female line, so Mr. McEwan's maternal connection to a clan which itself has no connection with Clan Ewen of Otter (see notes "Others joined..." and "MacDougal Campbell of Craignish" above, p7) can have no relevance to the question of whether the MacEwens 'are descended from different septs of the ancient Clan Ewen' as R. S. T. MacEwen claims here. There is in fact no evidence to support his assertions regarding common descent from Clan Ewen of Otter.

seals - In the following discussion, R. S. T. MacEwen fails to distinguish between heraldic seals made to denote a particular family or house, and ready-made seals suitable for common use.

Nisbet - Alexander Nisbet, 1722, *A System of Heraldry* (from the first page of the Preface).

in later times - Heraldic seals (to which Nisbet's remark above is relevant) were from the earliest times distinctive of a particular armorial achievement and were passed down from father to son.

father to son or heir. In some instances the devices were chosen as crests when a person of the name took out arms. The case of McEwan, Glasgow, is an instance in point. His arms were granted in 1847. The escutcheon displays emblems of his profession and pursuits, while the crest and motto,—an old stunted oak, putting forth new branches and fresh foliage, with the motto 'Reviresco,'—have been in use on seals by MacEwens everywhere from a very much earlier period. This seal has been used by individuals and families of the name in different parts of the country, in Argyll, Galloway, the Lennox, Renfrew, Glasgow, and other places, by persons who could only have recognised a clan relationship and must, personally, have been unknown to each other. It was evidently the emblem of the clan; a symbol of family kinship and clan origin which testified to common misfortunes and common aspirations. It was in use at a period long before the modern fashion of 'clan arms' and 'crests'—a custom without heraldic sanction—came into being, and was employed for purposes not of show and display but of business. The Lyon Office is unable to fix the origin or date of these seals, but states they are 'common to the name.'* So that this *quasi* heraldic device is another link between the past and the present of an ancient, shattered, but reviving race. For this is what the device and motto signify. It has been well chosen as an epitome of the history of the clan. It is not uncommon to find different families and members of different clans bearing the same crest, but there is no other instance of this device being carried except by MacEwens.

* See Note to Appendix.

This seal has been used - Elsewhere in the book, R. S. T. MacEwen notes only the seal used by Robert McEwen in High Mark, Galloway (d. 1860), which Mr. John McEwen believed to be 'of much older date'. There is no reason to doubt that Robert McEwen's seal was indeed of some antiquity, as it reflects his remote ancestry (see note "Reviresco" above, p18). According to family lore, the McEwens of Bardrochat had matching seals made in about 1830, at which time there was some uncertainty as to whether to adopt the crest and motto described here, or to adopt those registered by William Macewan of Glenboig. Unlike the Glenboig crest and motto, the Reviresco crest and motto were apparently not a matter of public record, yet must have been known as McEwen emblems in Bardrochat at that time—this may suggest a link with the Galloway family of High Mark who owned the original seal, and who are known to have had connections nearby in Barr and Girvan, Ayrshire. The next record of the Reviresco badge is in 1847 as the crest of John McEwan whose family was from Renfrewshire, and whose grant of arms seems to establish the tradition of MacEwen heraldry (see note "The three McEwen families" above, p35). All these earliest occurrences are confined to the south-western Lowlands of Scotland and would appear to indicate a highly localised tradition, which casts some doubt on R. S. T. MacEwen's assertion of its general use 'by MacEwens everywhere from a very much earlier period.'

the emblem of the clan - The crest described here is the traditional emblem of Clan Bisset (see note "Reviresco" above, p18) and now also of Clan MacEwen (see *Fig.8* above, p25).

'common to the name' - If R. S. T. MacEwen had enquired directly for information regarding these seals from Lyon Court, this answer could indicate simply that they were aware of their use among McEwans.

well chosen as an epitome of the history of the clan - The device was probably chosen to reflect the spectacular fall from grace experienced by Clan Bisset in 1242. No similar catastrophe occurred in the history of Clan Ewen of Otter—they simply lost their baronial status.

It is not uncommon - It is unusual for members of different clans to bear the same crest, but not unknown—thus, a boar's head erased proper is used by both Baillie and Breadalbane. A boar's head is a relatively common heraldic device however and, in this case, the combination of a very distinctive crest with an almost identical motto is highly remarkable.

there is no other instance of this device - The device is still used by Clan Bisset (see note "Reviresco" above, p18).

XI.—MacEwen Tartan.

Tartan has been the dress of the Celtic Highlander and of the Lowland Clansman from time immemorial, and particular 'setts' or patterns are of great antiquity, but it has been found impossible to assign dates to any of them. Distinctive clan tartans as now worn are of comparatively recent date In a work on Clan Campbell,* it is stated that "the adoption of peculiar tartans by entire clans is referable to the civil wars of the Earl of Mar and Prince Charles Edward, as the sources of the custom of wearing distinctive clan tartans." Long before that time we know from Logan and others that "every strath and every island differed from each other in the fancy of making plaids, as to the stripes in breadth and the colours, while family tartans were in a great measure dependent on individual taste." Since the abolition of the Act against the wearing of tartan, many old tartans have been revived, and in the present reign many new ones have been designed. The MacEwen tartan is a handsome blue and green check, with red and yellow lines alternately on the green bars of the check. It somewhat resembles the Farquharson and MacLeod tartans; or if in place of the white lines in the 'Campbell of Loudon' red lines be substituted, we get the MacEwen tartan exactly. The ground-work of the MacEwen tartan is the same as that of the 'Black Watch,' which was the original Campbell tartan. The MacEwen has the double black lines running through the blue ground as in the 'Black Watch,' the distinguishing feature between the two being that for the black cross lines (over-checks) of the 'Black Watch' there is a

* *The Clan Campbell*: J. Menzies & Co., Edinburgh.

Long before that - Although the notion that regional tartans preceded clan tartans would seem to be the new orthodoxy, it might never be possible to discover the truth of the matter. The earliest hints towards what might be considered clan tartans date from the seventeenth century, somewhat earlier than is suggested here, but it is highly unlikely that they were produced according to precisely specified setts as is the case with modern tartan patterns.

It somewhat resembles Farquharson - MacEwen tartan first appears in *Vestiarium Scoticum* under the name 'Farquharson'.

MacLeod - Presumably MacLeod of Assynt rather than MacLeod of Lewis.

Campbell of Loudon - MacEwen tartan is distinguished from this tartan only by its red stripe.

the original Campbell tartan - This tartan may have been adopted by Clan Campbell at the time of, or just after, the 1745 Rising. So many Campbells served in the British army that this must already have been the *de facto* tartan for the clan, but earlier portrayals of Campbells and associated clans show a variety of red-and-black tartan patterns. Clan Ewing tartan falls within this group of red-and-black tartans and is based on the tartan of John Ewing in Heiddykkis of Kirkmichael (d.1609) described in his testament as 'sax ellis of reid & blak cullerit claith' (six ells [= yards] of red & black coloured cloth).

red and yellow line alternately in the green ground of the MacEwen. The colours are brighter in the latter than in the former. In the work on Clan Campbell above referred to we are told that "the original name of the 'Black Watch' arose from the tints of their tartans, in which black and green predominated, as they yet do in those of the Campbells. The majority of the Western tribes, traceable all to one source, adopted nearly the same colours, and indeed there can be little doubt but that the distinctions now perceivable are of comparatively recent adoption. The 'Black Watch' tartan contains all the really fundamental parts of every variety of that species of garb. The difference of hues and the intermingling lines and divisions appear to be a later addition to the tartans of the separate tribes, and should be ascribed to the era of the later rebellions." The Campbells have had and still have several different "setts": Argyll, Breadalbane, Cawdor, Loudon, Strachur, and there may be others: but the late Duke of Argyll has gone back to the 'Black Watch' as the original clan tartan. The similarity of the MacEwen tartan to the 'Black Watch' and the 'Campbell of Loudon' (red in lieu of white lines) points to the early connection of the clan with the Campbells, just as in heraldry ensigns and cadences point to connection and distinction in families. In early times the tartan took the place of the heraldic shield.

points to the early connection - Although historical relationships can be written into tartans, it is not in any way a rigorous system comparable to heraldry. Only since 2008 has there been any regulation whatsoever of tartans in Scotland, and it is as likely as not that MacEwen tartan was assigned for rather more equivocal reasons, possibly by an agent for Wilsons of Bannockburn. After all, Clan Farquharson (the other clan associated with this particular tartan pattern) does not have any clear connection with Clan Campbell.

tartan took the place of the heraldic shield - This comment appears to contrast sharply with R. S. T. MacEwen's remark on the previous page, 'Distinctive clan tartans as now worn are of comparatively recent date'.

* Scale of Colours in MacEwen Tartan.

⅛TH OF AN INCH.	COLOURS.	⅛TH OF AN INCH.	COLOURS.	⅛TH OF AN INCH.	COLOURS.
3	Blue	6	Green	1	Red
1	Black	6	Black	½	Black
1	Blue	6	Blue	6	Green
1	Black	1	Black	6	Black
1	Blue	1	Blue	1	Blue
6	Black	1	Black	1	Black
6	Green	6	Blue	1	Blue
½	Black	6	Black	1	Black
1	Yellow	6	Green	3	Blue
½	Black	½	Black	...	...

For illustration purposes, suitable to the size of this volume, the scale of the tartan frontispiece has been reduced to about half usual size, such as would be worn for a scarf.

XII.—Summary.

The foregoing investigations and enquiries point to the following conclusions :—

I.—That Clan Ewen or MacEwen was originally a western clan, descended from the Siol Gillevray, one of the Celtic tribes of the Dalriada Scots.

II.—That they possessed territory, and were settled under a chief of their own in Argyll, on the shores of Loch Fyne, from the 13th to the middle of the 15th century, when the clan was finally broken up.

III.—That previous to the latter date they had suffered severely in the wars of the times, and both before and after the death of the last chief remnants

* This, and other information, has been kindly supplied by Mr. John C. M'Ewen, Inverness.

These details of the tartan were provided by Mr. John Cochrane McEwen of Holm Mills, Inverness. His family came from Neilston, Renfrewshire, and has owned the Isle of Muck since 1896. Modern custom is to describe tartan according to its thread count. With slight modifications for ease of comparison, the two earliest versions of MacEwen tartan as recorded at The Scottish Register of Tartans are:

Vestiarium Scoticum (SRT Ref: 1150):
Y8 K2 G44 K38 B32 K4 B6 K4 B32 K38 G44 K2 R8 K2 G44 K72 B6 K4 B6 K4 B56 K4 B6 K4 B6 K38 G44 K2

Clans Originaux (SRT Ref: 2427):
Y4 K4 G24 K24 B24 K4 B4 K4 B24 K24 G24 K4 R4 K4 G24 K24 B4 K4 B4 K4 B28 K4 B4 K4 B4 K24 G24 K4

(Y=Yellow : K=Black : G=Green : B=Blue : R=Red)

The thread count used as standard today is similar to the version in *Clans Originaux*, but omitting the original alternation between single and double black tramlines (SRT Ref: 2428):

Y/4 K4 G24 K24 B24 K4 B4 K4 B24 K24 G24 K4 R/4

The threadcount for Ewing tartan (SRT Ref: 11082) is:

R/12 K4 R48 K4 R12 K/92

I - We may agree that Clan Ewen of Otter was a western clan, as were the Galloway McEwens and the *Sliochd Eoghain* of Clan Cameron. Similarly, although the McEwans of Clan MacDougall looked towards Perthshire for their chieftain, the clan has traditionally reckoned MacEwens throughout Lorne, Argyll and the Isles as their own. The only surviving genealogy of Clan Ewen of Otter however contradicts any connection with Siol Gillevray or Dàl Riata (see note "sprung from the Dalriada Scots" above, p1).

II - R. S. T. MacEwen has failed to produce any evidence to support the suggestion that Clan Ewen of Otter was ever 'broken up'. It is clear that the Barony of Otter was ceded to the Campbells in the mid-fifteenth century, but there is no reason to imagine that this resulted in any break-up of the clan (see note "Sufnee or Swene, the IX. and last of the Otter chiefs" above, p6).

III - At the time of the wars which R. S. T. MacEwen suggests caused such suffering to the clan, Clan Ewen of Otter did not yet exist, and it is quite possible that the original Ewen of Otter had not even been born (see note "On the conquest of Argyll by Alexander II." above, p5).

sought new alliances and homes in Argyll, the Lennox Country, Dumbartonshire, Galloway, and elsewhere.

IV.—That at an early period of their history they became connected with Lochaber, if it was not (as Keltie asserts) their original settlement: that a second incursion took place from Lorne at a later period : that the settlers became incorporated with the Camerons, the principal clan in the district, and that the name of Ewen has been common among the Camerons and in the district from the earliest times of which there is any record.

V.—That the name is distinctly of Gaelic and clan origin, and that except where particular family histories and other evidence point to a different conclusion, persons bearing the name and traceable to the localities known to have been occupied by the early clan, its septs and descendants, are of the same race and probably sprung from the MacEwens of Otter. In the Lowland districts the blood has mixed largely with that of the Lowland inhabitants.

VI.—That, subject to the same exception, those bearing clan names in Argyll and the Western Highlands and Islands are presumably the descendants of the men who joined the Campbells and other Western clans, before and after the dispersion, in the 15th century.

VII.— That those traceable to the Lennox country, Dumbartonshire, the neighbouring Eastern and Southern Counties and Galloway are descendants of the Lennox and Galloway septs.

VIII.—That those traceable to Lochaber are more immediately descended from the '*Sliochd Eoghain*,' while those who settled in Skye may have had the

IV - Where the name MacEwen occurs in Lochaber it has no connection whatsoever with Clan Ewen of Otter, but has entirely separate origins. Keltie does not assert that Lochaber was the original home of the MacEwens and neither did any 'second incursion' take place from Lorne. The connection which R. S. T. MacEwen makes between Clan Ewen of Otter and Lorne is based on error compounded with error (see notes "On the conquest of Argyll by Alexander II." above, p5, and "MacDougal Campbell of Craignish" above, p7).

V - It is not possible to assume any connection between MacEwens in general and Clan Ewen of Otter. There is no evidence to connect the modern surname MacEwen with this particular medieval clan except in areas where the Ewing form predominates, whilst several alternative origins for the MacEwen name are clearly attested by reliable evidence. There is also evidence to suggest that the Lowland surnames Ewen, Ewan and Ewans might sometimes arise from English or Welsh origins. See note "Where the name is of clan origin" above, p31.

VI - MacEwens in these regions represent the same populations traditionally claimed to belong to Clan MacDougall. There is excellent evidence for the historical existence of the MacEwen name in Clan MacDougall, originating with Ewen Mor MacDougall of Ballinreoch, and this sept also extended into Perthshire (see notes "Perthshire" p28, "List of Persons Concerned in the Rebellion of 1745" p30, "the Muckly family" p35, "Muckly, County of Argyll" p44). Another group of MacEwens in Argyll and Lorne may be descended from the MacEwen bards (see note "hereditary bards" p8) and the possibility of descent from Ewen, King of the Isles, cannot be eliminated.

VII - There is no evidence whatsoever for regional septs of Clan Ewen of Otter. Whilst there is reason to believe that the Ewings of Dumbartonshire, Stirlingshire and Cowal may indeed be descended from Clan Ewen of Otter, evidence for McEwens in Galloway suggests that they are descended from Clan Bisset (see notes "the Black Douglas" p15, "McKeown" p17, "Reviresco" p18). Continuing links between Ewings in Dumbartonshire and in Cowal are evident in extant sasines (cf. Herbert Campbell, 1933, *Argyll Sasines*).

VIII - The words 'more immediately' serve no purpose here. The MacEwens of *Sliochd Eoghain* are so called because of their descent from Ewen McEwen Cameron of Erracht, and they have no connection with Clan Ewen of Otter (see notes "William MacEwan of Glenboig" p14, "the Erracht family" p20, "Sliochd Eoghain" p26, "Macewan of Glenboig" p35, "Glenboig, County of Stirling" p44). The MacEwens in Skye never existed (see note "Skye" p29).

same origin or have been descended from the men of Argyll.

The clan has had a hard and checkered existence from its earliest days; it was wiped out as a territorial clan in the middle of the 15th century. From that date it has been scattered in groups in different parts of the country, the largest number having migrated to the fertile regions of the South, where the clan names are now more numerous than they are in the Highlands. In this respect the history of the clan is not exceptional. It is more remarkable that, considering its early dispersion and subsequent vicissitudes, it is still possible to speak of 'Clan Ewen.' Few clans can offer such scanty material to their would-be historian. Clan Ewen was broken up as a clan during one of the darkest ages of our history, when chroniclers were few, and such an event was too common to excite their interest. In later times the evidence of family papers and contemporary records is singularly scanty; even family and local traditions—those unfailing resources of the clan historian—are all but wanting. In other clans allegiance to a recognised chief has been and still remains a powerful bond of union; but it would baffle the patience of the most unwearied genealogist to discover on whose shoulders the mantle of the lords of the Otter has now descended. More tantalising still is the absence of personal records. Now and again some ancient document gives us a list of names; but what manner of men these were, of what physical or mental complexion, we can but dimly imagine. The scenes which the lurid light of Privy Council records reveal to us tell of the licence of an age rather than of individual character, and if there were some who "preferred the mischevious and un-

a hard and checkered existence - Clan Ewen of Otter suffered a loss of status through the loss of the barony of Otter which would undoubtedly have affected clansfolk and tenants, and, although the names Eugenius and Ewing do appear in Cowal after this, they do not seem to occur within the the barony of Otter. According to tradition, the clan relocated with its chief to the area around Loch Lomond (see note "under a chieftain of their own" above, p12). This move would have been planned and negotiated in the years preceding Swene's death. Life was generally tough in early modern Scotland compared with the way we live today, but there is no reason to believe it was significantly tougher for our own ancestors than it was for their neighbours.

it has been scattered in groups - R. S. T. MacEwen restates his belief once more but, throughout his entire booklet, he has failed to provide evidence to support this belief, and has ignored or been oblivious to substantial evidence which would contradict it.

It is more remarkable that - This is in itself another argument against R. S. T. MacEwen's viewpoint. It is highly unlikely that a clan name could have survived into modern times without the conventional structure of a real clan to support it and give it meaning. If clansmen adopted new allegiances they were by default adopting a new clan and, unless they formed a substantial community with its own chieftain, they would simply have been absorbed within the clan. Even in its heyday, Clan Ewen of Otter was not a large clan, and it is not possible that all MacEwens have inherited their name from this clan.

Clan Ewen was broken up - There is no evidence whatsoever for the break-up of Clan Ewen, nor any reason to believe that such a break-up ever occurred (see note "Sufnee or Swene, the IX. and last of the Otter chiefs" above, p6).

family and local traditions - This book has preserved three or four accounts recorded from such traditions, and for these traditional accounts we owe R. S. T. MacEwen a debt of thanks.

a list of names - Lists of names which happen to include a random 'MacEwen' are of no use in constructing a history. Many such documents list members of a single clan so, since most of these men share the same clan name, they are identified in the list by their patronymic. Anyone whose father was called Ewen will appear in the list under the name 'MacEwen'.

happy course of bypast wickedness," there were others —bards and senachies and honest gentlemen—who sought "godliness, civilite, good reule, and quietness." But despite lack of chief and lands and ancient records, Clan Ewen still preserves—if not its unity—at least a sense of union and clanship.

At the present time there are many bearing the Clan name in Scotland and in England and the Colonies. Some are men of affluence and property; many hold prominent and influential positions in the learned professions, the army, commerce, and agriculture. If the descendants of the ancient Clan Ewen could be mustered to-day they would make a a goodly show as compared with the "200 fighting men" of old.

a sense of union and clanship - Everyone of course recognises a sense of fellowship with others who share the same surname, but the true spirit of clanship is based on shared history, shared allegiance and ultimately on shared kinship. R. S. T. MacEwen devoted this book to his claim that MacEwens shared more than the name, but was unable to provide evidence to make good his assertion. Indeed, there is clear evidence for separate MacEwen origins in Clans MacDougall and Bisset, which between them probably account for most instances of the surname MacEwen in modern Scotland. There is also evidence that some MacEwens may be descended from other clans including Clan Cameron and, as in the case of R. S. T. MacEwen himself, Clan Ewing (see note "there is no memorial" above, p13). See note "Where the name is of clan origin" above, p31.

the ancient Clan Ewen - Although other MacEwen roots may be equally ancient, the 'ancient Clan Ewen' referred to here is of course Clan Ewen of Otter. With the loss of the barony of Otter, the clan appears to have largely relocated to the area of Loch Lomond and Dumbartonshire in the fifteenth century (see notes "Sufnee or Swene, the IX. and last of the Otter chiefs" p6, "under a chieftain of their own", "in the fifteenth century" p12). The chief of the Dumbartonshire clan was granted arms in the name of Ewing in 1566, and its descendants are represented today by Clan Ewing (see notes "under Lennox", "where they received a banner" p12, "there is no memorial" p13, "all the arms of the later Ewings" p35, "a hard and checkered existence" p41).

"200 fighting men" - See note "200 fighting men" above, p5.

APPENDIX.

Arms pertaining to Persons and Families bearing Clan Ewen or MacEwen names, as recorded in the Lyon Court of Scotland.

NAMES.	ARMS.
EWING (on a tombstone in Bonhill Churchyard, 1600. Supposed to be Ewing of Craigtoun).	A chev. between three stars, with the sun in base.
EWING (Keppoch, County of Dumbarton, descended of Craigtoun).	Ar. a chev. embattled az. ensigned with a banner gu. Charged with a Canton of the second, thereon a Saltire of the first, all between two mullets in chief, and the sun in his splendour in a base of the third. *Crest*: a demi lion ramp., in his dexter paw a mullet gu. *Motto*: Audaciter. *(see illustration on page 33.)*
EWING (Glasgow, descended of Keppoch).	Quarterly, first and fourth, as the last, within a bordure az.; second and third, ar. a bend gu. between three banting birds ppr. for Bontine. *Crest* and *motto* same as last.
EWING (Levenfield, County of Dumbarton).	Ar. a chev. gu. ensigned with a banner of the second, charged with a Canton az. thereon a Saltire of the first, all between two mullets in chief, and the Sun in his splendour in base of the second, a bordure indented, also of the second, charged with three crescents of the first for diff. *Crest:* a demi lion ramp. holding in his dexter paw a mullet gu. *Motto:* Audaciter.
EWING (Loudon).	As the last, the bordure charged with three mullets az.

Bonhill Churchyard - It is possible that R. S. T. MacEwen had direct knowledge of this tombstone, or that he was told about it by his correspondent in Luss (see above, p13). A somewhat different account is given by Bishop Alexander Ewing (1814-73) who visited Bonhill in 1844 in search of his Ewing ancestors, but found little of interest 'all the graves of the Ewings of Balloch having been built over when the new parish church was erected, with the exception of an Alexander Ewing, on whose tombstone the family arms were sculptured, and who must, from letters in my uncle's possession, have been a first cousin of my grandfather' (*Memoir of Alexander Ewing*, p101). Although this stone is not now visible, it is probably covered only by a thin layer of turf.

Keppoch - The Ewing family of Keppoch is ancestral to (not descended from) Ewing of Craigtoun (see note "all the arms of the later Ewings" above, p35). These are the same arms as recorded in the Workman Armorial in 1566. The saltire is not shown in the original illustration, but this may simply be due to the scale of the drawing (cf. R. R. Stoddart, 1881, *Scottish Arms*, which reproduces the manuscript illustration). Likewise, the Workman Armorial does not record the crest and motto, but these were presumably identical with those later used by the Ewings of Keppoch, who claimed the undifferenced Ewing arms. See *Fig.1* above, p22, and *Fig.7* above, p25.

Glasgow - Alexander Ewing, 1869, *Lyon Register* Vol.VIII

Levenfield - John Orr Ewing of Levenfield, 1870, *Lyon Register* Vol.VIII. The Orr Ewings make up a distinct group within Clan Ewing, and their crest is distinguished from other Ewing crests in that it is armed and langued Azure.

Loudon - William Ewing of the City of London, 1870, *Lyon Register* Vol.VIII

William McEwan M. P., 1886, *Lyon Register* Vol.XI: 'Gules a Garb Or on a Chief Argent a Lion's Head erased of the first armed and langued Azure' *Crest*: 'the Trunk of an Oak-tree with a branch sprouting forth on either side proper' *Motto*: Reviresco. See *Fig.5* above, p23.

Charles Lindsay Orr Ewing, 1893, *Lyon Register* Vol.XIII: 'Argent a chevron embattled Gules ensigned with a Banner of the second charged with a Canton Azure thereon a Saltire of the first all between two Mullets in chief and the Sun in his splendour in base of the second a Bordure indented also of the second charged with three Martlets of the first for difference' *Crest*: 'A Demi-Lion rampant Gules armed and langued Azure holding in his dexter paw a Mullet also Gules' *Motto*: Audaciter.

Robert Finnie McEwen of Bardrochat, 1908, *Lyon Register* Vol.XIX: 'Quarterly, first and fourth, Or, a lion rampant Azure gorged with a ducal crown proper, on a Chief of the second three garbs of the field, for McEwen; second and third, Gules, three headless cranes Argent, as Arms of affection for Finnie' *Crest*: 'the trunk of an oak tree sprouting proper' *Motto*: Reviresco. See *Fig.6* above, p23.
The crest and motto of Robert Finnie McEwen, 1908, would appear to be identical with those of William McEwan, 1886, although their family lines are not directly related. See *Fig.8* above, p25.

NAMES.	ARMS.
EWING (Ballikinrain, County of Stirling).	As Levenfield, the bordure charged with three mullets ar.
MᶜEWAN (Mackewan, Muckly, County of Argyll, descended of the Macdougals of Lorne).	Per fess az. and or. in chief a lion ramp. ar. gorged with an antique crown vert. in base a garb of the first.
MᶜEWAN (Macewan, Glenboig, County of Stirling).	Ar. a Sheaf of arrows p pr. banded az. between four roses in a Saltire gu. *Crest:* a dexter arm coupled at the shoulder, the elbow resting on the wreath and grasping a scymitar all ppr. *Motto:* Pervicax recti.
MᶜEWAN (Glasgow, of a Renfrewshire family, descended on the female side from a daughter of Campbell of Craignish).	Az. on a fess ar. between a lion ramp. in chief of the second, and a garb in base or., a ship in full sail on the sea between a thistle and a stalk of sugar cane, both slipped ppr., a bordure gyronny of eight of the third and sa. *Crest:* the trunk of an oak tree with a branch sprouting forth on either side ppr. *Motto:* Reviresco.

Ballikinrain - Archibald Orr Ewing of Ballikinrain, 1870, *Lyon Register* Vol.VIII

Muckly, County of Argyll - John Mackewan of Muckley, 1743, *Lyon Register* Vol.I. For Muckley, which is in Perthshire not Argyll, see note "the Muckly family" above, p35. The entry in *Lyon Register* (I, 376) records that John Mackewan was 'Great grandson to Ewan More Mcdougal of Ballinreoch, brother to Mcdowal or Mcdugal of Lorn ...' so it is from Ewen Mor MacDougall of Ballinreoch that he and others of his sept take their name. Ballinreoch is near Ballinluig, also in Perthshire. See *Fig.2* above, p22.

Glenboig, County of Stirling - William Macewan of Glenboig, 1796, *Lyon Register* Vol.I. Glenboig is in Lanarkshire, and should not be confused with Easter Glenboig, Middle Glenboig and Wester Glenboig, near Fintry, Stirling (see note "Macewan of Glenboig" above, p35). The sheaf of five arrows is a traditional symbol for the five branches of Clan Cameron, and is now used as the crest of Cameron of Lochiel; the old Cameron crest was identical with that adopted by William Macewan of Glenboig as described here. William's full achievement appears on the bookplate of George Macewan, preserved in the Brooking Rowe bookplate collection (No.1303). See *Fig.3* above, p22.

Glasgow - John McEwan, 1847, *Lyon Register* Vol.IV. John McEwan's crest is not tinctured Proper ('ppr.'—i.e. in natural colours), but Vert (i.e. green). The illustration shown below this entry on p44 (opposite) does not show the arms described; see *Fig.4* above, p23.

R. S. T. MacEwen was unaware of two early seals described in *Scottish Armorial Seals* by William Rae Macdonald, which was also published in 1904:
No.898 is for Thomas Ewen. Although Macdonald gives the surname as 'Ewing', the name on the seal is actually 'Euyn'. In surviving documents marked with his seal dated between 1532 and 1543, Thomas's surname is spelled variously as 'Ewine', 'Ewin' and 'Hewyne'. Thomas lived in the east and his descendants are more likely to go by the name 'Ewen', 'Ewan' or 'Ewans' than the modern surname Ewing which originates in the southwest of Scotland (the '-ng' ending was already established at this date, but cannot reliably be used to differentiate families). Thomas Ewen's seal shows 'Three lily heads stalked and pendant with a cinquefoil in chief' and may be compared with similar shields belonging to families named Evance, Evans, Evayne, Ewen and Ewens in England and Wales, where the lilies are replaced by their usual heraldic equivalent, the fleur-de-lis (cf. William Berry, 1828, *Encyclopaedia Heraldica*, vol.II; Joseph Edmondson, 1780, *A Complete Body of Heraldry*). Shared heraldry may denote shared ancestry, and points to an origin outside Scotland.
No.1061 is for Mariota, daughter and co-heir of Malmoran of Glencharny, wife of Nivin Mac Ewyn, and is attached to a document dated to 1365. Mariota's seal shows an impaled shield, with the chevron of Glencarnie (her father's shield) on the left, and three birds (presumably for her husband's shield) on the right. Although it has not been possible to discover the identity of Nivin Mac Ewyn, Mariota's known geographical links are with Strathspey and Strathearn—it is tempting to speculate that she might be related to another Mariota Euyn, McEwyne or Barron, who appears as a landowner in Tullich, Elrig and Moniack in 1547 and 1555 (NAS GD176/53-4, GD176/72). The device of three birds is reminiscent of heraldry connected with Cairns, Glenn, Rutherford, Houston and Makgill.

Heraldic encyclopaedias sometimes list arms for an Irish family of Ewing. The crest seems to have first been mentioned in *British Crests* (Alexander Deuchar, 1817) and the shield in *The British Herald* (Thomas Robson, 1830). These arms do not appear in the *Register of Arms* in the Office of the Chief Herald of Ireland.

NOTE.

All the Ewing arms are founded on those of the first Ewen or Ewing of Craigtoun. He belonged to the family of Keppoch in Dumbartonshire, and by marriage with the eldest daughter of Bryson of Craigtoun obtained that estate and took the arms of Bryson. The other Ewings obtained grants at different and later dates, founding them on those of Craigtoun, with the proper heraldic differences.

The Muckly (Argyll) and McEwen (Glasgow) families both claim relationship to Lorne families which were joined by MacEwens of Otter.

The Glenboig (Stirling) family belonged to the Lennox sept, as also did McEwan, Glasgow.

McEwan, Glasgow, took for his crest and motto a device and motto which had been common to MacEwans everywhere for a long time previous, and had been used as a badge on seals, of which there are specimens extant in MacEwan families. The Lyon Office states they are 'common to the name.'

A coat of arms is the exclusive property of the grantee, and descends to his eldest lineal representative. Younger children are not entitled to their father's arms, but are required to 'matriculate' them in the Lyon Court with their proper differences.

A modern practice has arisen of assuming 'clan arms' and 'crests': it has no heraldic sanction and is absurd on the face of it; because arms were originally the devices by which one person was known from another when in armour, which would lose its purpose if everybody had the same arms on his shield: it follows that members of a clan are not entitled to use the arms of the chief.

On the subject of crests, Woodward in his work on Heraldry has the following: "In Great Britain the crest has become the part of the armorial insignia most generally employed. We find it divorced not only from the coat of arms but from its helm, doing the duty of a badge on furniture, plate, buttons, panels of carriages, the harness of horses (and he might have added note paper). It need hardly be said that all this is an entire departure from the original idea of the crest as the ornament of a knightly helm; and that to speak (as people who ought to be better informed often do) of a whole achievement,—arms, helm, crest, and motto,—as "our crest," is as absurd as it would be to call a suit of clothes a tiara." These crests are really the work of the modern 'heraldic' stationer.

the first Ewen or Ewing of Craigtoun - R. S. T. MacEwen is mistaken in this assertion. The Ewing arms are first recorded in 1566 in the name 'Ewing' without territorial designation (see note "Keppoch" above, p43). The Ewings of Craigtoun inherited the undifferenced arms of Ewing from the Ewings of Keppoch.

took the arms of Bryson - The Bryson arms are not in any way connected with the arms of Ewing (see note "belonged originally to Bryson of Craigtoun" above, p34).

Muckly (Argyll) - Muckly is in Perthshire, not Argyll. See note "the Muckly family" above, p35.

joined by MacEwens of Otter - There is no evidence for any links between these families and Clan Ewen of Otter (see notes "On the conquest of Argyll by Alexander II." above, p5, "Others joined …" and "MacDougal Campbell of Craignish" above, p7). Even if R. S. T. MacEwen had been right about this, these maternal connections would not be relevant to the origin of the family surname, which is inherited through the paternal line.

Glenboig (Stirling) - Glenboig is in Lanarkshie, not Stirling. See notes "William MacEwan of Glenboig" above, p14, "Macewan of Glenboig" above, p35, "Glenboig, County of Stirling" above, p44.

common to MacEwens everywhere - The only early example of this crest and motto used in conjunction with the MacEwen name comes from Galloway, where there is reason to believe the McEwens are descended from the McKeowns or Bissets of Glenarm. Both crest and motto are also recorded for the Bisset family (see notes "the Black Douglas" above, p15, "Reviresco" above, p18).

'clan arms' and 'crests' - R. S. T. MacEwen is correct to say that both shield and crest belong exclusively to the individual armiger, but it is now an established custom that clansfolk wear a badge showing the chief's crest surrounded by a strap and buckle bearing the motto. Whilst these clan badges may only have taken their present form during the lifetime of R. S. T. MacEwen, the tradition of heraldic badges stretches back to medieval times.

On the other hand individuals, families, members of clans, may use a badge if they desire to use a distinctive mark. This was a common practice in ancient times, the device and motto being displayed in seals. Woodward says: "Badges were the earliest form of hereditary insignia, preceding shield or coat armour, and commonly used as seals. It was distinct from a crest, although family badges were sometimes used as crests. It is described as a subsidiary family ensign, occasionally accompanied by a motto, borne by adherents (clansmen), dependants, or retainers. It is entirely different from the species of badge, unrecognised by heraldic authority, which has gradually sprung up among the Highland clans, namely a leaf or sprig of some tree or shrub, usually carried along with two eagle's feathers in the bonnet which the Chief wears."

The MacEwen badge was probably one of these old statutory seal badges described by Nisbet, who says it was enacted by sundry statutes that every Freeholder should have his proper seal. It had to be produced when required at the head Court of the Shire, and duplicates in lead were often kept by the Clerk of the Court for reference in case of need.

A badge differs from an armorial crest inasmuch as the latter nearly always rests on a cushion, whereas a badge has no cushion, and the seals almost invariably bore the initials of the owner for the time being.

A badge may always be used as a mark of distinction if people desire it, but it should be distinguished from an armorial crest. This badge is not a crest except in the single instance of McEwen, Glasgow, who chose it for his own, and as such it belongs only to his representative; but as a badge it is common to all clansmen. As such it is more interesting and valuable than any modern crest; for it is not a borrowed ensign or assumed plume, but an original, ancient, and unique device, containing an historical epitome, which crests do not.

a leaf or sprig of some tree or shrub - The use of clan plant badges is often claimed to be of ancient origin, but is as likely to have been a more recent attempt to develop clan badges without infringing the heraldic rights of the chiefs, or simply a way to affirm a link between the clans and an earlier way of life closer to the natural world.

The MacEwen badge - R. S. T. MacEwen is referring to the sprouting oak stump which featured on the seal of Robert McEwen in High Mark (see above, p18) and which has long been used as a crest by the Bisset family (see note "Reviresco" above, p18).

every Freeholder - The McEwens in High Mark appear to have been tenants not freeholders, so these legal requirements would not have applied to them.

rests on a cushion - This probably refers to the torse or wreath (in some cases replaced by a fillet, chapeau or coronet) which was designed to cover the attachment of the crest to the helm, and which usually appears below the crest in illustrations. The torse is not an intrinsic element of the crest itself, and its absence cannot be considered a reliable distinction between a crest and a badge.

single instance - A similar crest was also granted to William McEwan, 1886 (*Lyon Register* Vol.XIX), and has since been granted to Robert Finnie McEwen of Bardrochat, 1908 (*Lyon Register*, Vol.XIX).

as a badge it is common to all clansmen - This device is undoubtedly a crest, but the crest badge (displayed within a strap and buckle bearing the motto, cf. *Fig.8* above, p25) may also be considered 'common to all clansmen'.

any modern crest - The ancestors of the Galloway McEwens have probably used this crest and motto since the thirteenth century and, as such, it has a deeper association with their family history even than their surname.

www.ingramcontent.com/pod-product-compliance
Lightning Source LLC
LaVergne TN
LVHW091552070426
835507LV00010B/805